Conversing on a Higher Level

by

Ellen Marie Blend

A LeasCon Book

Copyright ©️ 2001   by Ellen Marie Blend

All rights reserved by U.S. Government Copyright laws. Published in the United States by Image Ink Publications.

Copy edited by Pamela M. Green
Associate Editor Toni Rodgers

Library of Congress Number: 2004102888

ISBN: 1-929219-04-0

First printing: June 1, 2010
Second printing: July 2017

Copies of this book may be obtained through major bookstores, website: http://www.ellenblend.com, or by contacting: editor@ellenblend.com.

Dedication

This book is dedicated to Mike, who unknowingly but perhaps willingly was a conduit to serving a communication on a higher level. He probably had agreed to take on the assignment before coming to earth, but since we normally do not bring this memory with us, was unaware of his spiritual purpose to himself and to me.

Throughout the writing of this book, I had tried to reason what our purpose was in being placed together. I very much knew upon our first meeting, as did he, that it was with definite purpose. It was a contrived meeting by a higher power and not by chance. I was given many signs, some very explicit. It is within the pages that follow that I try to uncover and restate the missions given us, the karma that has had to be worked through, and the answers to questions I would never have expected to be answered through Mike.

Mike unknowingly allowed the soul of another to share space with his. He was sent to me for the purpose of completing another's karma, and I was sent to him to help him grow and gain stability. I presume that Mike is at a very early stage of a series of lifetimes on earth. There are times I would swear he was just born yesterday with the limited life experiences to which he related. He is clearly at the beginning of his journeys. He has so much to learn, and yet has a great deal of spiritual awareness. I sometimes wonder if he was sent from another planet mainly for my purposes. My friend, Gwenn, always said that she felt he was from outside of this hemisphere; just one of those physic intuitions of hers.

I will let you decide for yourself on this matter, but I am certain that the missions presented to us have been fulfilled.

CONTENTS

Introduction

Most of us have lived many lives before and will live many lives again. Some may be closer to completing their karma of a combination of lifetimes and not need to return to earth while others will complete, if successful, their karma for this life. Some of us are guides for others on this earth and some are here as angels who point out what might otherwise be missed. Those same angels may have other guides here for them, or other angels to give them a spoken word. Spirits, guides and angels abound. It is only those who are clearly and succinctly alert, who believe and take note of the signs, who see this truth.

What is true for me may not be true for you. You may not have experienced the same unveilings as myself. Our lives are full of experiences, some experiential, and not all of us recognize them. Therefore, we will not reach the same plane at the same time. Some will never reach a higher plane in this lifetime.

Life is a huge stage of characters who play out their roles and interact with one another. What is to happen is just as much a mystery to them as it is by the best writers and playwrights of all times. Even as I watch the events unfold, know that there is a purpose for each happening, and choices by many to be made that determine each outcome, I am in awe. I quote about life from someone who reacted to a series of events that had just happened: "Isn't it great theatre?"

Body, Mind & Spirit
Books by Ellen Marie Blend

Visual Encounters
Unraveling The Weave
Looking Back
Impunity from Lunacy – Book One
Impunity from Lunacy – Book Two

Watch for These Titles Coming Soon

When Is It My Turn?
Real Objectivity
Spiritually Speaking
Your Chosen Path

Also Written by this Author

Not About Money
Her personal story of a corporate career, the decline of morality in corporate America, and a prelude to automotive bankruptcy

The Educator
Countless Ideas to Teach Students How to Think

Chapter One

Balancing the Rods

Lillian and I returned to her home after going out for dinner one evening. She carefully made her way from my car, up the three stairs, and to her doorway. Her stocky body, long swaying hair and jovial nature made up her personality. Lillian was always fun; even going to the grocery store with her was fun. She made it that way because she lacked a very important attribute of her being—her eyesight. She was legally blind, and was told that her lack of sight was caused from previous incarnations and that she now needed to find inner peace.

I had accompanied her into her bedroom wherein she began rummaging through one of her drawers. A picture of her lover stood upright on her chest of drawers. At this time, she had not explained what it was that she was looking for or what we were going to do. She found one piece of bent wire, asked me to hold onto it, and then searched for the second one. When found, she handed it to me to carry, one in each hand.

She had a set of L rods, also known as divining rods, which were meant to give yes and no answers to questions asked of them. The rods would mysteriously move in or out determining one's answer.

I recognized them as something I had seen used several years ago. A former neighbor's profession was putting in septic fields, and he had helped locate underground water on my property with a set of rods made from coat hangers. I saw them work for him, and tried them out myself. They worked for me as well, but when my husband tried the exercise, he was unable to get any reading. The neighbor explained that not all people were able to use them successfully.

In carrying Lillian's L rods from her bedroom to the living room, they reacted wildly. I could not control them. They continually thrashed in movement from an open to closed position and then open again. At that time I still did not know what it was that we were going to be doing with them.

She first held the rods in her hands to demonstrate their use and explained what to and not to do. She said that it was important to be nice to the rods in asking them questions. She asked them to please give her the answer to the question that she asked. She spoke sweetly and softly to them, as if play acting. I was to take in this information quite seriously.

It was sort of a superstitious ritual, but one which I treated with respect; however, I was unable to follow through with such painstaking kindness--I was just matter-of-fact with them.

She demonstrated in this way. She stood in front of me, holding the rods outright, and pleaded with them to show her what action of the rods would indicate a yes, and then a no. She commented that the actions portrayed might be different for me. When asked for a yes, the rods crossed over one another tightly, and when asked for a no, they opened up wide, unable to touch one another. I had the same response from them when it came to my turn.

She held the rods first and had me ask yes and no type questions, to which we patiently awaited the rods' indication of an answer. I felt as though my privacy would be invaded if I were to ask personal questions, so I resisted asking that type of question. Next it was my turn to hold the rods and she would ask her questions.

She had me hold one rod in each hand, the short end of the L in each palm, with thumbs up. The long end of each rod extended out about 12 inches. It was important that one stand erect as to not tilt the rods in either direction.

This time she asked the questions while I held the rods. This was thought not to influence the answers, as it was clear that the rods' direction could easily be manipulated by a tilt of the body.

One of her questions was in regard to our current President and his most recent exploitation of being accused of involvement in an affair with a certain lady. I had already confirmed in my mind that he was guilty, as a matter of common sense, and it was clear that she had pre-determined his culpability as well. However, when asked the question as to his involvement with the lady, the rods clearly stated no, to our disbelief. The actual testimonies that followed also indicated his innocence, which wavered on a fine point.

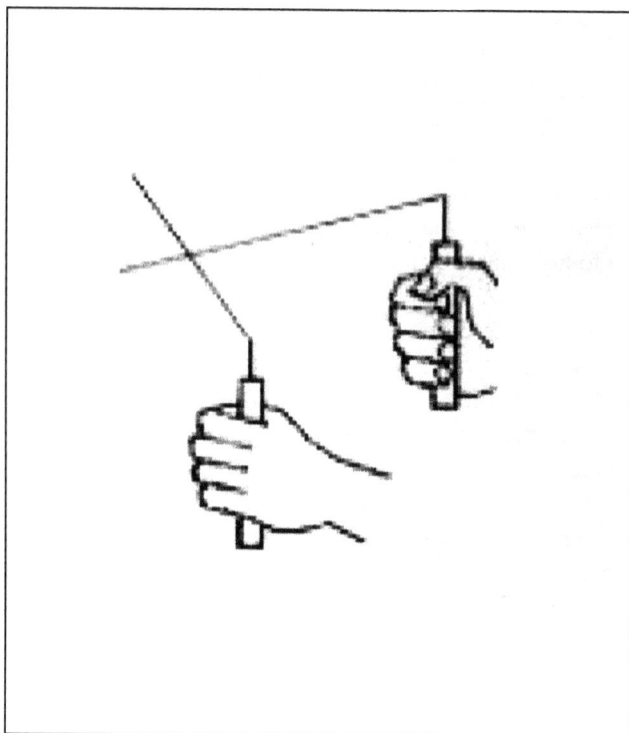

L-Shaped Divining Rods

We then moved toward more personal questions. Both of us were interested in being pursued by gentlemen for meaningful relationships, so it was probably no surprise that I asked the question, "Would I meet someone meaningful in my life by June 1 of that year?" This time we experimented with holding the rods ourselves and asking the questions. With great hesitation before answering, the rods indicated yes. Since they were confined to these simple yes or no answers, I suspect that my answer was really "Yes, but . . ."

1) Yes, but maybe it won't be good,
2) Yes, but maybe it won't be what you want,
3) Yes, but maybe there will be more than one,
4) Yes, but maybe there is much, much more to explain.

I somehow felt that there was a hidden agenda.

I wasn't convinced of the seriousness of these rods, but I did find them to be interesting. They offered some type of intrigue, and since I was entertained by the experience of using them, I commented that I would like to have a set of my own.

With that, Lillian immediately went to the telephone and called her friend who had gotten them for her. She put me on the line to talk with him. He gave me the telephone number of the Society of Dowsers, and an explanation of how to describe the Dowser Rods so that I could order my own set.

I ordered them, and also obtained their catalog of many such items and books of information on the like. The catalog showed other forms of similar tools such as Y rods and pendulums.

There were several books and pamphlets offered in which I had an interest. The catalog explained the origin of the dowsing rods and how they had been used over time. I found other information on things like intuition, finding water, body aura, thought forms, undesirable energy, earth energy, and numbers and dates.

I told Gwenn, a close and informative girlfriend, of ordering a set of these rods for myself. She accepted the idea as a good experiment for us to try. She also related that someone in her family had used a Y rod or divining rod.

When my son and his girlfriend came over, I let them experiment with the rods. They came to the drawn conclusion that there was no validity to them and that the answers were foregone conclusions which one could manipulate in body movement by pure thought. I was inclined to believe that was probably true, and discarded the thought that there should be any seriousness associated with them.

A few months later, Gwenn brought forth more information. She had just seen a program on television about such rods, called dew rods, where a scientific explanation gave validity to their use. Dew rods got their name when used to find water. Gwenn thought it was stated that the following experiment was made in Seattle.

The program commentator stated that scientists had traced magnetic lines in the earth with the use of dew rods. Where multiple lines had been found to cross, say five or six, there had been high levels of energy found. These dew rods were used in tracing these magnetic fields, and it was thought that where the fields crossed, electro-chemical reactions occurred.

Further, persons who felt particularly troubled were thought to be out of sync with the magnetic fields of the earth. In medical terms, this would compare to a person whose synapses were misfiring and causing them mental duress. It would be the same as having a spine out of place and not being in harmony with the body. It was thought that a visit to these particular sites on earth could result in realignment of oneself with the earth, thus putting the body back in harmony.

Chapter Two

Choices of Fate

When Matt and I separated, for what was to be an interim break, we actually came in contact with one another on three occasions personally, and twice telepathically. He lived quite far from me, an hour's drive, so the crossing of our paths was somewhat extraordinary.

The first time an opportunity was given to us to make amends was obviously up to me, but I didn't feel that it was. I had seen Matt no more than two car lengths ahead of me in traffic, and elected to turn off so as not to meet up with him. I had felt it was his choice to leave the relationship, so there was no point in my trying to circumvent his wishes. In hindsight, since our positions on that road were such that I was to see him and he not see me, this was my fateful choice. I suppose I might have tried to reason with him regarding the value of our love, but my feelings had been scarred and I didn't feel it was my place. Pride was also a factor.

The second chance meeting was at my house, in the backyard. He had dropped by my next-door neighbor's house on business during the afternoon, when I normally would be working, and did not expect me to be home at that time. He did try to communicate with me, but everything he said, which was to be light, but personal, conversation infuriated me more. I left him standing there and went inside. It was clear that he still wanted to keep distance in the relationship, and that only hurt me more. That occurrence was obviously his choice.

On the third instance, I again saw him in traffic. It was a day that I had left work early and pulled out of the parking lot gate directly behind him in traffic. Fate worked its hand with extreme precision. He could have been in the next lane, or a block up or back; but no, he not only was in the lane into which I must enter, but the light had changed to red and we were stopped. We were forced to notice one another, and this time we both took fate's opportunity to pull off the road and engage in conversation.

It was obvious that no love had been lost over time by either of us, but he was not ready to surrender his position in the break in the relationship. He held his ground firmly. This meeting was followed with a couple of loving and emotional phone conversations.

The timing was just preceding his birthday, and though I hoped and probably prayed that he would offer to spend his birthday with me, as he did many times before, he was not willing. In the next phone conversation, he actually broached the subject of us getting back together. "It would be so easy to come back right now," he said. And then he asked if he should.

I felt that the timing may be premature to his purpose of separating, whatever that was, and my heart too bruised to trust that that would be a good idea. I told him that he didn't have to decide right then; I couldn't decide. That time fate gave us each a choice, and we still failed. The uncertainty left us both without a firm decision, and no action resulted.

The next points of communication were made telepathically. I had gone on with my life and had met Steve, who had already moved into a small portion of my heart where Matt had left a void. When my feelings began to deepen for Steve, I telepathically asked Matt what I should do. He answered telepathically that he would always be with me, and that I should just go on with my life.

However, when the realization of the depth of my new heartthrob reached Matt, telepathically, he cried out to me for guidance. He asked me if he should come back.

Two things were at play. I knew that he would only be coming back because he felt the pain of my straying feelings; he had not completed whatever it was that he needed to do in order to feel comfortable in the relationship. It would have shortcut the process. The second thing at play was that feelings for Steve kept getting in the way. I therefore told him that if it was not right to come back now that he should not. I also told him that I loved him dearly, and that everything would be all right. That was the last opportunity that we had to decide on our relationship.

In time, Steve also took a sabbatical from me. With a pending divorce, an ill mother, and a change in job location, he thought it would be better to resume our friendship in the fall of the year.

Chapter Three

Whirlwind Affair

It was Saturday night, and I did not have a date. I had been out the evening before to a singles dance on the west side of town and had met two new gentlemen, both of whom had taken my phone number. I made a date with one of them for the following weekend.

I had worked around the house all day and had made tentative plans to go out with Kristen, one of my single girlfriends, and was looking forward to going out. However, by evening, Kristen did not care to go out. For whatever reason, I was determined to go to a local restaurant, By-the-Bay, that had dancing that evening, or perhaps to another singles dance on the east side where I lived.

I dressed to go out for the evening. I felt determined to do so, but I didn't know why. It was normally not that important to me to go out one way or the other. The day before, a co-worker had said that he was going to take his wife to dinner at By-the-Bay on Saturday, and knowing that I frequently went there, said that maybe he would see me there. If I went there, I would have someone to talk to, and some excuse for being there by myself. This in itself would be quite unusual, even perhaps out of the question. It was not a normal thing for me to do, but I was on my way, propelled by some force to get there.

Choices. I still had choices. When I exited the freeway, traffic was so heavy that I was unable to make a left hand turn, the direction I would need to go for By-the-Bay. I sat there, behind another vehicle trying to turn left also. This vehicle gave up and turned right. I then waited in cue. No break in traffic availed itself. I, too, decided to turn right. Turning right would be the direction I needed to go to attend the singles dance.

I turned right, judiciously juggling my choices. After turning right, I found a place to make a U-turn and was on my way to By-the-Bay. I entered the bar from the back area, furthest away from the dance floor, and walked slowly through the crowd looking for anyone that I might know. This was the first time I had ever entered such an establishment on my own and did not feel uncomfortable. Normally I would be uncomfortable even if I had agreed to meet someone there and had arrived first.

I rounded the bar to where the dance floor was and the band was set up, and as I passed the mid-point, a friendly soul approached me and gave me a bantered remark about a vacant seat for which we were both about to volley. He was not shy, and had no qualms about taking over the seat, leaving me to stand next to him. He remarked on how his legs were bothering him and how much he needed the chair, so naturally, I had no argument.

Conversation was underway, and before long he ordered a pricey hors d'oeuvre for us to share, asking for my recommendation. My normal shyness escaped me, and I actually asked him to order me a glass of wine. I couldn't even believe my own boldness, much less his. For whatever reason, this approach seemed to go smoothly, and the entire evening progressed into more conversation, eating, drinking, dancing and laughing.

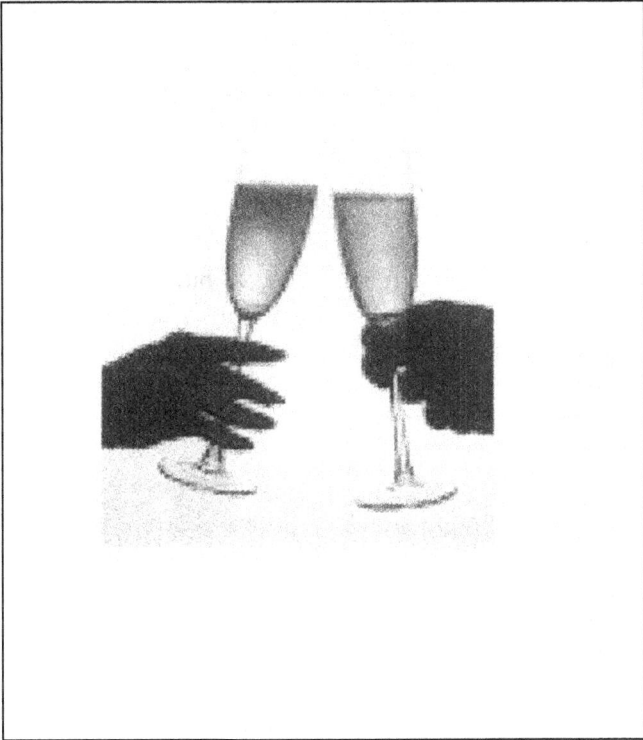

The Sharing of Wine

Feeling conspicuous for being there by myself, I explained how I had anticipated meeting up with a friend and his wife from work, but had not seen them. By then I had perused the crowd and had assumed that my friend's plans had changed.

By the end of the evening, I had learned a little bit about my new friend, Mike, and found that he lived on the west side of town, quite inconvenient from me, and that he was interested in seeing me again.

His height and size were very comfortable for me. His demeanor and ease of verbalization were uncannily similar to Matt. However, I immediately recognized this personality as potentially being bi-polar. Or, as I call it, manic, because it cloned the symptoms that I knew so well. I even asked him if he was, but he declined to counter with any acknowledgement as to what I was talking about. This was not being evasive on his part, or trying to deny it; it was just not ever a consideration or thought to him. But, I highly suspected it.

Despite his character being very much like Matt's, he reminded me of my friend, Frank-O. His voice and manner were hauntingly like someone I thought was from some television show, but since I was not a watcher of TV, was not able to identify the actor. When he suggested he might be reminding me of a personality from some movie, I had to really think about it. At the end of the evening, I confirmed it was Gene Wilder. He even looked a little like him. His facial expression, voice, and smirky smile were identical. He was adorable.

We made a date for the following weekend, but mid-week he asked to come over for a drink after getting out of work. I was anxious to see him. His remarks, in jest but real were, "I can't wait to see you. . . , like I really mean I CAN'T WAIT." I thought he was so cute, looks and personality, that I was more than happy to oblige. I had admittedly told my friend, Mary, that I already missed him, and it was only a few days since meeting him.

As we talked more and I became more informed about his interests and background, I realized that I was reliving a portion of a combination of male persons of my past. He told me that he loved to dress up, as did Matt, and I already knew that his personality was very much like his. Undeniably so. He reminded me of Frank-O, whom I already have surmised is someone from a past life, and he placed his hands in my pockets, something Steve liked to do, and told me how much he loved music, as did Steve.

"What are you doing to me?" I asked God. "Why have you sent me this man?" Particularly, why did you send me a cookie cutter mold of Matt?

Unmistakably, even though Mike knows nothing of the other men in my life except Matt, whom I cannot deny his likeness, a known fact to us both is that this meeting between us was *not by chance*. This meeting was with purpose from the heavens above, with deep and undeniable emotion, and was moving forward in a whirlwind fashion.

It was with a stretch on both of our parts to be at this meeting place at that particular time. He was way out of his work territory, and had gotten very lost on the way. He had driven about 30 freeway miles past his destination, and was just as determined as I was to get there. What was driving him to go there that particular evening? And I, to enter an upper echelon establishment by myself.

After the second meeting, I confided in my friend, Gwenn, that I was really enjoying this man, mostly because of feeling the comfort in his likeness to Matt, but that I did not see this as a permanent relationship. I related that I felt it would make for a wonderful and fun summer.

As author Penny Thornton said in her book, *With Love from Diana*, "At one time I would have recoiled at the notion that fate was a powerful force in my life—or indeed, anyone's life . . . But over the years, my experience as an astrologer and the extraordinary way my own life has unfolded has taught me otherwise. There are times when I know that in every fiber of my being that I have been guided to be at a particular place at a particular time. From that point an elaborate fabric of events is woven that eventually makes a small piece of history. In some cases that history is relevant only to the few people directly involved. It has no place in the great scheme of things. But in some cases, a small piece of history has a much wider impact."

End of week two. This is a whirlwind affair!

Chapter Four

Ride Sally Ride

On our first weekend date, after the mid-week meeting at my house, we had gotten together fairly early in the afternoon. He had told me previously that he would be moving during the day and would have to work that evening, so our meeting would be rather late, after 9:00 p.m. I was amenable to any schedule, a direct relation to my complacency in life at the time. However, he decided not to report to work until Sunday, having such flexibility, and come over early.

It was a beautiful day, which allowed us to sit in the backyard, have something to drink, and enjoy the sunshine. My house afforded a lake view, and we looked out at the water and watched the boaters. It was late in the afternoon when he called to announce his early arrival, which was about 45 minutes from then. I was just finishing an outdoor painting project, had not showered or washed my hair, and was not alarmed by my shortness of time to get ready.

I completed my work and cleanup, washing out the paint brush, roller and paint pan, and then went in the house to take a shower and wash my hair. I very well could have blown my hair dry with a hair dryer and rolled it quickly in hot rollers to accomplish being ready on time. However, I put on my makeup, set my wet hair in rollers, and chose to have my hair dry in the sun and fresh air. That is how I was when he arrived. I did not question what his reaction to this might be. It felt quite comfortable.

He was amused, but was also as comfortable as I. I proceeded to polish my nails at the outdoor patio table as we conversed, feeling just as natural as if we had been dating a year or more.

When my hair and nails were dry, I finished getting ready for the evening. We went out to dinner, and then came back to the house. Still with complete comfort with one another, we later decided to go out again to another place for dancing. My area is populated with places having music and dancing.

We had a great time. The music bordered on old pop songs and some trendy blues, which we both seemed to enjoy. We danced a few times, and particularly enjoyed dancing to an old song, "Mustang Sally," in which the chorus repeats, *Ride Sally Ride*.

We were the only ones on the dance floor, and while others surrounded us at tables and bar rails, no one joined us. In fact, even though we were making a bit of a scene having such a good time, Mike commented the next day that no one smiled or paid particular attention to us. "It was as though we were transparent, did you notice?" Yes, I had noticed. I thought this to be a little peculiar, too.

"I've always been on my own dance floor, anyway," he commented. A very manic statement, I thought.

This skillful, maneuvering salesman managed to convince me that he should stay the night and that nothing would happen. He did, to my equal enjoyment, and nothing did happen. He was a healthy male, but a gentleman. How bazaar an occurrence this was. Rollers in my hair and then an overnight stay? There was no getting use to each other. We were as comfortable together as if we had lived together for years.

This next week brought a holiday weekend, and with the relationship with Mike so new, I did not know entirely what to expect. I was waiting for him to indicate that he would like to see me more than Saturday, since we had Sunday and Monday off from work, but he said nothing.

So, Mary and I took advantage of an invitation to go sailing for the weekend. While on the trip, Mary grew concerned with regard to my relationship with Mike, and how I might be conducting my future time. She didn't want to lose my friendship and our ability to do things together.

"Looks like you are going to have to make a decision pretty soon," she said, recognizing the seriousness of my involvement so soon.

"Like what," I asked, already knowing what she meant.

"Well, as to whether you will be seeing Mike exclusively or dating others as well." This question was with the unsaid words, "Are you going to have time for me?"

21

"Oh, I said. What's to decide? It's here, and I just plan to *enjoy the ride."*

I was going to a barbecue at my son's house that following afternoon, and had already nearly finished packing for this overnight sailing trip that Mary and I had managed to pre-arrange. It was Memorial weekend, so returning on Monday afternoon still left a little time for Mike and I to get together in the evening. I was to call him when I got back home.

I figured that I would have an hour to get ready before he arrived, so I called him just as quickly as I could after arriving home. While I was still on the telephone with him, he told me to look out my front door. He was in my driveway. How romantic he was, and how anxious he was to see me, as I was to see him.

I still had to get cleaned up, and he settled himself in the living room to watch television while I unpacked, had a bath, and got ready for his company. It was as if we had been doing this for years.

In conversation about each of our previous evenings, I had told him about the entertainment in the bar where Mary and I had eaten and had a drink. "The guy played Mustang Sally," I said. "*Ride Sally Ride*."

"I heard it last night, too, and thought of you. I haven't heard that song in thirty years! Now you're telling me you heard it last night, too?"

"That is just too bizarre," I said. "There must be a message in that for us." I then remembered my comment to Mary, "I'm just going to *enjoy the ride*."

Mike and I were both very intent on the fact that we had been thrown together for some purpose, and that perhaps we had lived together before, in some other lifetime, to be as comfortable as we were together. And to be so deeply emotional about each other was another factor. We were very much aware.

I just heard a message on the radio, a sign, perhaps, that went like this:

> The opportunity that God sends does not
> wake those that are asleep.

One must be awake and alert to catch all of the signs, and know that there is a purpose. Another sign followed shortly.

This week I was at my computer doing some writing, and used the word excursion. I then questioned its appropriateness where I had used it and used the available computer Thesaurus to check its synonym. To my surprise, the word *sally* appeared. It said:

Sally: To rush or leap forth suddenly. To issue suddenly from a defensive or besieged position. To make an attack upon an enemy. An excursion. To emerge spiritedly, as from a resting place. A quick witticism or bantering remark, a quip.

It was as if God was saying, *just enjoy the ride*. I have been giving you signs. "Did you get it? Bong! Here it is again. Did you get it now?"

Okay, okay, I get it! *Ride Sally Ride!*

I shared this information with Mike and we discussed it openly, laughing. The next time we went out for a drink, we toasted to the pleasure of our new relationship, and *To The Ride*!

Chapter Five

The Sphere

In keeping with my usual in-depth look at people, this whirlwind relationship has me searching. Gwenn asked if I had taken what we have learned to call a reading of Mike, which meant had I looked for a symbolic image of Mike's inner soul. I explained that a vision had tried to appear a couple of times, but that I hadn't allowed it to come forth enough to determine what it was.

During the brief interlude that Mike was away from me this weekend, working, I was tired enough to stop everything and lay down on the couch to rest. It was then, when the mind slowed down enough to cleanse itself of the busyness of the day, that I settled into a meditative state to see the formation take shape.

The third time, now, I saw an oval shape appear. It was like an upright football, in a skeletal structure of generously spaced wire rods from top to bottom. It revolved, or rotated on its axis. Now, what was it? I had no idea what to call it. I guessed I might have to sketch it for Gwenn, and surely she would know what it was.

A sphere, I thought, but never being quite sure of myself, pulled the dictionary from the bookshelf and looked up the word. I was hoping for a picture, but there was none.

A Sphere

It said: Geometry. A three-dimensional surface, all points of which are equidistant from a fixed point. A spherical object or figure. A planet, star, or other heavenly body. In ancient astronomy, any of a series of concentric, transparent, revolving globes which together were thought to contain the moon, sun, planets, and stars. Celestial. The environment in which one exists, acts, or had influence; range; domain. One's social stratum, rank, or position. To surround or encompass, a ball, or globe.

This was it. It was three-dimensional, all points equal distance from a fixed point, a globe of sorts, and it revolved.

When I told Gwenn of my findings, she identified it with something in space, not originating from this earth. "Extraterrestrial, she said." She was psychic in her own realm.

"How's celestial?" I asked.

"Okay," she agreed. "But I still say it's from outer space, out of this world, out of this hemisphere." Note that hemisphere is half a sphere.

We talked at some length trying to figure out the purpose for this relationship. I could somewhat see my purpose in his life. I felt that I was here to give him the quality of life that he was now looking for and the solace he so much needed.

What the purpose for me was, I didn't know, but I was sure that there was one. He's an angelic body to me, a beautiful person. I adore him.

Isn't it somewhat uncanny that name of the first American woman to go into space was Sally Ride? That was June 18, 1983.

Chapter Six

Short Term or Long Haul

I had been telling Gwenn how I felt about Mike, how endearing he was to me, and in such short time.

"Of course," she said. "Why should this surprise you? You already are aware that you have lived together before at some time, and that is why you are so comfortable together. There should be nothing strange about that."

"I can't begin to tell you the depth of emotion we both feel," I continued. "It is clearly there on both our parts, and has not had the time to develop."

"That's because it was there before, and this is just an opportunity for you to complete whatever was not completed right in another life," she said.

Mike keeps telling me how baffling this experience is to him as well. He continually asks himself, "What are you doing? This is crazy." He admits that he cannot shake the fact that he is drawn to me, and that he tries to reason with the fact: "I miss that girl. I really miss her."

I miss him, too, when we are apart. Very strongly and I did, right from the start.

"Somehow I have the feeling that this is not going to last," I told Gwenn, "but I don't know why. I just feel that."

"You might be right. You have that physic sense."

"I could be dead wrong, though, I really don't know."

"*Ride Sally Ride*," she said.

"That's right. That's my sign."

Contrarily, this relationship and its emotional depth is exactly what is so extraordinary and precious. This is the very substance that is so necessary for a perfect union. We already have it and do appreciate it. I continued my conversation, with feelings still gnawing at me.

"I don't think we will separate on bad terms. I just think circumstances will be there where a decision will have to be made, and that will separate us."

"Maybe."

"Gwenn, I can't tell you how emotionally sick I felt when the thought crossed my mind that something would separate us. Mike and I were talking about his job, and the thought occurred to me that when he gets this promotion within the next 90 days, that the company might transfer him and whisk him away from me. I became so emotionally sick."

I told that to Mike, as I can tell him anything, and he said, "I wouldn't let that happen. I have a choice, too. And I would never take you away from water. You have to be located on water like you are now. However, if I get offered a job on some island again, as I did before, I might take you with me."

This relationship is two weeks old. Can you even fathom such deep emotion and understanding? Such far-reaching thinking? It is here and real.

"Maybe that's what happened in your last life together, and that is why you feel that sickness so strongly," Gwenn suggested.

"Well, if it did happen, I already know I would say, "Go. That is what you are supposed to do."

"Maybe that is what you need to do in this lifetime—to let him do what he needs to do. Maybe you didn't let him go last time, and that is why you will have the opportunity again."

Gwenn was always giving me input, scenarios of what might or might not be. How she peaked my imagination and rationalism.

"I don't know if I am in this for the short term or the long haul," I continued, "but I still feel that if someone like Steve came into my life, it would still cause me great consternation."

"Oh, really," Gwenn said.

"Yes. Steve did something for me that Mike cannot. Steve made me feel wonderful and beautiful, maybe because he was so good looking. Do you think so? Our connectivity was much different. It was not nearly as easily defined. Actually, it is still an unknown as it has not been given the opportunity of closure. And on the other hand, Steve would never be able to give me what Mike does."

"That's because you have a different karma with each of them," Gwenn said.

Mike and I can reach such depths, I thought. Soon I know I will have the ability to reach his very soul, as I had been taught so well by Matt. My total well being will shortly be in his entire control because he takes me so deep. I will lose control. I know that and also know that he will take good care of my soul. I have no doubt about that. I also suspect that his soul is just as out of control as mine.

I recalled Gwenn's words. She had given me an assignment, as she often does. I had told her about Sabrina, a co-worker and friend, now deceased. She read Tarot cards and told me the reason for my failing marriage.

She had said to me, "I will read your cards for you. I never charge for this. I feel that I have a gift, and if I can help you, that is what I want to do. I know when I have hit on something, and it is the right answer, because I get goose bumps all over."

In my reading of many years ago with Sabrina, during the time of my failing marriage, she got the goose-bump card. She hesitated, still thinking, and said, "Wait, this is it. This is very important." A moment passed.

"Your husband feels less worthy than you. He cannot tell you this because he does not know. That is why he continually eats to satiate his inadequacy and why he cannot lose weight."

My marriage failed due to his obesity. I was totally appalled by his appearance and rejected having him anywhere near me. That was most unfortunate, as he was really a good man.

Gwenn and I got goose bumps when we hit upon a scenario of how Mike and I might separate. Her synopsis was that what I probably will need to do in this lifetime is to let Mike grow emotionally independent from me.

When I asked Gwenn if she thought I had a lesson to learn in this encounter, she said, "Tonight when you go to bed, ask Sabrina. She is your guide. She will be the one who can answer you."

I talked to Mike for about an hour after this conversation with Gwenn and fell directly to sleep when going to bed. This assignment will have to wait for an appropriate time.

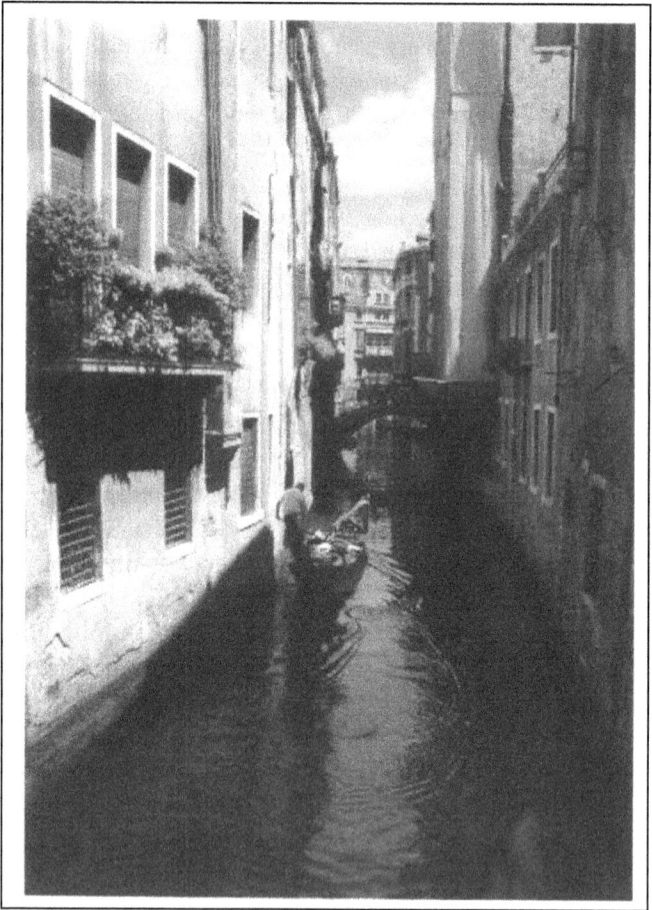

Venice, Italy

Chapter Seven

16th Century Venice

"I feel like I've known you for a thousand years," Mike said.

"You have," I responded. "We just have to figure out where and when."

"It was Venice," he countered. "16th Century Venice."

"Is that why I've always fantasized about Venice?" I asked. In truth, I always have. I've never fantasized about anything else in my life, but I've always had some fascination with Venice.

He continued. "It was 16th Century Venice, and I was serenading you. I had my guitar, and I was singing you a song."

I could see myself looking down from perhaps a second story window to the dark waters of the canal, and listening to my loved one sing to me. He was so romantic. He was courting me, perhaps trying to entice me into a marriage encounter.

In reality, I never could understand anyone who fantasized about anything. It was so unrealistic, and I was so down to earth. Why would anyone fantasize? Reality is where it is, where it should be. But I had fantasized about Venice.

In jest, he continued, "I was in my canoe, and I was singing to you."

"It was a gondola," I laughed.

"Oh yes, a gondola. It was a canoe," he corrected.

One might think this very juvenile to even question the validity of such a fabrication. I, too, would agree. However, I must question, is this just one more subtle sign? A message? Could it be true that we once shared a life in Venice many years ago?

Chapter Eight

Drawn in Like a Magnet

From the very start, I was drawn to this man. I kept telling Gwenn that I did not feel sexually attracted to him, so it wasn't that, but I was very much drawn to his very being, his character and personality—like the force of a magnet. He excited me, and I missed him when I was separated from him like I've missed no one else before.

In the very short time that we have been together, three weeks now, we have discovered that we have very similar tastes and values. I guess that discovery is not too different from any other new couple who are finding out their reasons for compatibility.

Of the more silly things to muse over, we both love music, dancing, coney island hot dogs, cookies, salads, and tomatoes on sandwiches. We are both upper middle class, and quite unpretentious. Neither of us has any mechanical or simple fix-it abilities and don't have the patience to close a zip lock bag. We don't find making a perfect bed a necessity or within our ability, and we both leave partially used tissues in specific places throughout the house.

One of my biggest concerns is knowing that this man is manic, and I question if this is a good idea for me. Severe manic depressives can be risky people to have in your lives, and are potentially dangerous to themselves.

I spent fourteen years with Matt, clinically diagnosed as bi-polar, or manic depressive, and would not have turned him away. After that many years, I felt that I knew what I was dealing with.

I also knew that severely depressed people suffered from ultimate despair and a feelings of no hope. They were also capable of committing suicide. The actions of a manic depressive are not always predictable.

Now, here I was with a carbon copy of a Matt personality. It was so identical that I knew Mike's every move and his every need. To be debated is the fact that manic depressive people can have a wide range of highs and lows. I never found Matt to suffer from any deep depression.

In conversation with Mike this past weekend, I explained to him that he was most definitely manic, even though he had never been diagnosed as such. I hated to be the one to break this to him, but I was now absolutely certain.

"Is that bad?" he asked.

"It probably won't hurt you. There are some very wonderful qualities in manic persons. They feel things more deeply, have more passion, are generally happier, and my guess is that you don't ever really experience lows."

"Why is that?" he inquired.

38

"Well, I'll tell you what a therapist told Matt, and your personalities are identical. Matt was told that he continually experienced his highs and lows within the same moment, and since he never experienced either separately, he was unaware of them."

"Oh, rapid cycles," said Mike.

"Yes. And since you are very well adjusted, and comfortable with who you are and being on your own dance floor your whole life, it probably will never hurt you."

An example of manic behavior, to which I was very well accustomed, was this. Mike was working on Saturday and called to let me know how his day was going and the time he expected to be free to come over. He had just made an offer to a homeowner, whose home he was in while selling, of a trade of some entertainment books in exchange for a chair for his bedroom. He had just loaded this chair into his car, so I would see it when he arrived.

By the time Mike got to my house, the chair had been traded for a bouquet of roses for me. This series of events was a perfectly normal occurrence in the life with Matt, so I was not surprised of the events leading up to the gift of roses. It was just another day. Did it hurt anyone? It was perfectly harmless, abnormal behavior. It was manic!

Sunday brought another series of fun events, where quiet little me became the manic. We had had one of those storybook kind of days. We had awakened together, each requiring about an hour of sleepiness over a cup of coffee to wake up and start our day.

I had thought to begin my day's activities with planting some flowers that I had brought home the day before, when it occurred to me that it would be fun to get into the hot tub on my back deck before getting cleaned up. This suggestion was met with pleasure by Mike, so I poured   each of us a glass of orange juice, and we proceeded to enjoy it while relaxing in the hot tub.

Afterwards, we each got dressed for the day. I planted my flowers while he read the newspaper. Then Mike suggested that we go out for some Sunday afternoon fun at a local place that had afternoon music. It was another place on the water, with an outdoor patio and indoor restaurant and pub. The music had been moved inside due to the coolness of the weather, so we were happy to sit inside.

We ordered a late lunch and listened to the music. Exercising my new forwardness, it was I who asked Mike to dance. I explained that he should be prepared to see that only he and I would be on the dance floor, as it was unlikely that others would dance in the afternoon.

He, like me, never minded being the only ones on the floor. We danced by ourselves, only joined by a lonesome fellow, or perhaps mentally challenged, who loved to dance too and danced by himself. This was odd, I agreed, but I have been seeing more and more lone, strange dancers lately. The band enjoyed our taking pleasure in the music and did not hesitate to comment on the lovely couple on the dance floor. They tried to encourage others to join us, but had only a couple of takers.

"That's why I need someone like you," I said to Mike, meaning a man who was more extrovert than not.

Imagine that! I couldn't. I had just said that I *needed* someone like him, with his manic personality and characteristics. Amazing. I astonished myself.

I was just as much amazed that I too often opened my mouth to express my feelings openly to this man. I told him how much I missed him. I told him when I *wanted* him. This was not only not like me, but I did it with such ease and comfort.

Had I experienced so much with this man in a previous life that it was second nature to me now? Is that why all of the formalities are gone? Is that why they are not needed?

Mike commented to me as well of the unrestrained feelings he had in luring me into bed, and this was in week one. He remarked how forward this was of him, and how he really didn't want anything to happen so quickly. It was just a natural feeling he had in wanting to be with me.

Had we already been there? I think so.

Chapter Nine

444 LUV

As previously indicated, I am able to see visions of people's spirits, or symbolic replications of their being, indicating what is going on in their lives. I also recognize signs and messages in many things that I see and do. When I receive this symbolic information about someone, I must interpret what it means.

When I first began to see this information I would ignore it, but I don't ignore it anymore. It's kind of like having conversations with God. How many people do you know that read license plates on the cars in traffic and get messages? I've done this for several years now.

Paying attention to these signs, I have noticed that license plates with letters or numbers in three's, or at least two's, have been appearing quite frequently. I have been unable to decipher any meaning from them just yet, but interpretation has always been difficult for me.

This repetition has caused me to wonder what it is all about. I've tried to think of things that are usually thought of in three's, with Gwenn's help, like Mind, Body and Soul, or the Father, Son and Holy Ghost, but I've had no confirmation as such. No goose bumps, either.

Still, they continue to appear before my eyes, not letting me know what is meant by them. In more simplistic terms, since they normally relate to persons in my life, I wonder if the letters and numbers are about the men I have loved. I try to rationalize if two means both Mike and Matt, and the three pertains to Mike, Matt and Steve.

It is very uncommon that I would feel a real love for three male persons within a three-year period. That is a most fortunate experience for me, or for anyone, for that matter, since many spend years looking for love.

Understandably, I nurtured a deep love for Matt having spent all of those years together. He is the soul that recognized me from a past life, although it was not a topic for either of us at the time and was never discussed. I just recall his conversations at the beginning of our friendship, which tells me this is so. I did not know how to read signs at that time, and past lives, soul mates, or any clairvoyance were totally unknown to me.

Then Steve came into my life, and I soon recognized his soul. I think he recognized mine also, but did not know what he recognized. As said by another author, Brian Weiss, in *Only Love is Real*, "One may recognize a soul mate from another lifetime and the other not, leaving that person to go on without the other." I definitely felt a love for him as well, and now he has gone on to someone else, leaving our relationship without closure.

I then recalled a conversation I had with a young lady who asked me for some personal advice in regard to an unfinished relationship in her life. She had related that she was heartbroken at his leaving her, but now was involved with someone else and happy. Now that the first boyfriend wanted her back, she was torn as to what she should do.

She continued. "He wants to get back together with me. There was a time that I would have given anything for him to say that, but now I'm kind of content with my new friend. What should I tell him?"

"Don't tell him no, or never, just not now. If he really cares, he will wait."

I don't know where the wisdom came from, but I felt sure about this advice. I wondered if I might someday be faced with the same circumstances should Steve return in my life.

In regard to Mike, I don't know that either of us recognize each other's souls, but we are both quite certain that our meeting was destined to be. It was very purposeful and probably timely. We just don't know what the purpose is, why, or why now. We most definitely are aware that some very strong forces were at play to bring us together that first evening under some very awkward and constraining circumstances.

As each day passes with my relationship with Mike, I wonder at what point I will not feel the remembrance of Steve so strongly. Steve was so important to me, and I had felt that we were somehow connected. I feel that Matt and I are through for this lifetime. My thoughts are that whatever was not completed will have its opportunity in some other lifetime.

The last license plate that I read gave me clear definition of the signs that I had been seeing. It read 444 LUV. I knew that it was directed at me because of the 4's. My birthday is the 4th day of the month of the year 1944. This was the spirit world's way of telling me that I was experiencing the love of a third very important man in my life.

So new is this relationship with Mike, that I cannot realistically understand why I already feel a love there, but I do. Mike feels it, too. He has not said this to me in so many words, but he has related it in repeating a conversation to me that he had with a friend.

He said, "I didn't expect to fall in love with this lady, but I have."

I'm sure its foundation goes back a thousand or more years.

Chapter Ten

Parallel Planes

Gwenn has been a dear friend for many years. She and I met through a temporary work experience for me. I had been laid off from a major corporation, and had taken a volunteer job with a Chamber of Commerce office that my company had done work for. Gwenn had been working for this office part time, but needed full time work. She then hired into the corporation that I had been laid off from as temporary help, but maintained a one-day-a-month assignment with the Chamber office as a boardroom reporter. That's how we met.

While the closeness of our relationship did not develop for many years, today we are in constant contact and maintain steady communication. We have a wonderful friendship, and speak with complete openness and confidentiality. We are spiritual guides to one another and, more remarkably, she is an interpreter of many of my life's complexities and esoteric, supernatural visions.

While many friends experience parallels in life, we may have encountered them in similar ways, but not necessarily at the same time. This gives us a basis of equality and understanding.

Gwenn is currently reading a book written by Shirley MacLaine, and is comparing the characters in the book to the relationship I have with Mike. There are two lovers who recognize that their meeting was not by chance, and they are on a roller coaster ride romance. *Ride Sally Ride*.

This is not the first time that Gwenn has picked up corresponding information to my life either at a church lecture, something she has seen or heard, or a book she has read. The timeliness is always profound, and certainly not accidental. She is my guide on earth.

The two lovers in the book are paralleling the emotions of Mike and myself, and the growth of their love is just as quick and spontaneous. A revelation in validating the purpose of her reading this book at this time follows.

Gwenn left a message on my work voicemail, bringing me up to date with the happenings in the book. She told me that the romance was going fine. She then asked, "By the way, how is your sugar level? Were you having any problem with it yesterday? I have to know."

She was aware that I have low blood sugar, and when I eat too many sweet foods or sugar-filled drinks, I get very lethargic and just want to sleep. The tiredness gets so great that I can hardly move. While I have learned to control it for many years, I occasionally slip up, and the symptoms can erupt suddenly. This hasn't happened to me for many months, perhaps even more than a year.

I responded, also by message, as she was working away from her office that day, "Yesterday I was fine. Today I am having an awful time. I'm going to have to go on a diet of red meat for a few days to pull out of it. Why?"

When we finally spoke to one another, she told me that the woman in her book is also experiencing a sugar imbalance at the present time. I asked her to read the last chapter so that I would know what is supposed to happen, but she did not agree to do that.

Having the experience of other spiritual guidance that Gwenn has offered in regard to events in my life, I have learned that she will present the right information when it is time. Whatever is going to happen in my relationship with Mike, I will receive pertinent information that will follow along the same path as the characters in the book that Gwenn is reading.

Gwenn tells me that she knows that it is her job to guide specific persons here on this earth, not just me. That is her purpose. That is why many times my visual imagery of her, in spiritual form, is of that little angel who flits from place to place sprinkling magic dust from her wand, and touching the lives of all those who depend on her help.

Chapter Eleven

Developmental Love

This is week three of the relationship. I knew during week two that I already felt love for this man. I had to evaluate carefully if I was re-living the love I had for Matt in Mike, with them having such similar characteristics.

It is true, the reason for feeling love so soon had to be related to my feelings for Matt. Each man had such depth, and were each able to verbalize their emotions, although Mike is much less protective of his feelings. That may be because of a confidence we both share in the relationship. He tells me that I do not resemble or remind him of anyone else in his life. The relationship between Matt and myself took years to develop, so I don't know why Mike would feel love for me so quickly other than a past-life experience.

I also find Mike to be very well adjusted. He has endured many hardships, some very recent, and two failed marriages. I don't know the reasons yet, but his comment is that every hardship makes him stronger.

Now for the fun in the relationship. Hockey season is in, and Mike has asked me to be his hockey buddy. It is so nice that a man can share this manly game with a female and feel so comfortable. He bought me my own Red Wing hat, and I am now into it. The team is in the final running for the Stanley Cup.

Last night, by invitation, I met Mike, his daughter, and daughter's boyfriend for her birthday celebration. I was glad to be included in this family celebration. Mike's daughter was adorable. She talked incessantly, with happy little chatter, and was most likeable. Her boyfriend, with whom she lives, seemed to dote on her. He was a good looking, quiet young man, and would have to be in order to be compatible with her. I enjoyed meeting both of them.

Mike was his usual gregarious self, and had no doubt filled his daughter in on our meeting and expeditious relationship. He did not hold back how many times we had spent the night together in only three weeks, nor the fact that we had planned some near-term vacation time together.

He humorously remarked, still in disbelief of the rapidity of events: "Three weeks! It's only been three weeks!" We both shake our heads in total amazement. The comfort level goes beyond twenty years.

A hockey game was on in the restaurant where we met, and at one point his loud and voicetress reaction of cheer to the team was excessive. He apologized for being overly exuberant. I was not offended by the outbreak, and it was fun to see him getting into the game.

When his shouts of approval continually happened, he asked, "Will you still love me if I keep having these outbursts?"

I smiled, motioning my head up and down slowly. I was saying yes in acceptance and also in admittance to his candid question.

"How do you know that I love you?" I asked.

"Because I love you," he frankly replied.

Chapter Twelve

The Beat Goes On

Never have I been so tired in my life. My rest time has been minimized and my sleep pattern utterly destroyed. I can hardly keep up, but will not give up an opportunity to see Mike.

Since he works evenings, making sales calls, and I days, getting home around 6:00 p.m., our schedules are not conducive to a convenient relationship. I have about three hours to get the mail in, feed the cat, straighten out the house, and sleep for a fast hour so that I can meet Mike after 9:00 p.m.

An hour's sleep makes me feel like it's a brand new day, and I'm ready to roll into the night. I've been returning home about 11:30 p.m. to get some more fast sleep, and I am up again at 5:30 in the morning to get ready for work.

The weekends are also filled sharing time with Mike. Because he works evenings, I usually have Friday to myself to meet with my friends, although he sometimes tries to rendezvous with me later in the evening.

If not, his arrival on late Saturday afternoon is much awaited, and having the early part of the day to clean house and do outside yard work has worked well. We cannot be separated again until the weekend ends.

I cannot explain where all of the emotion has come from so quickly, but it is definitely there on both of our parts. That makes it all the more beautiful. When apart, we both deeply miss one another, with that hollow, emptiness eating away at us. With only one day apart, it is essential that we meet again to re-energize through our embrace and fill the emptiness with love.

I had talked to Lillian, the lady with the L Rods, regarding our future engagement for dinner. She said that she had some exciting news to share with me, and I then told her of my new relationship with Mike. I explained how he was such a copy of Matt, and how I anticipated his every need, move, and thought. "He is an exact duplicate, other than looks," I told her.

"How can that be?" she asked, surely doubting my evaluation.

"I don't know," I said, "but he definitely is. I've even asked God what he is doing to me. Why did he send me another one just like Matt?"

A smirk of uncanniness and a hum precipitated through the telephone line. She no doubt did not agree with my assessment, but reserved further comment.

"We'll talk more when we get together," I said. "I'm anxious to hear of your news as well."

"Oh," she said, "mine is not of that nature. It's about my music."

"That's great," I confirmed, "We'll get together on Friday.

In a quick conversation with Gwenn mid-week, I told her of the events and happenings to date with where Mike and I were in the relationship. She interjected her thoughts and brought me up to date with the lovers in the book that she was reading, and gave her thoughtful comparison and analogy to where Mike and I were at this time.

She stated that the couple in the story were still doing well, correlating the events that Mike and I were sharing. They, too, were so astounded by the quickness of the development of their relationship, and also believed that they had been together in some past life. They decided to go to a channeler, or someone clairvoyant, who could give them insight.

"Gwenn," I said, "we are going to have to get together soon. You're going to have to tell me everything you know and have read about split souls."

"Why's that," she inquired.

"Because I think that is what I'm dealing with. How else do I have a human body that has the same soul as Matt? It's an exact duplicate."

"Interesting," she said. "I'll be anxious to learn what the couple in my book find out. That may give some insight into your relationship."

"Yes, it might.   We're into the love part now," I explained.

"Oh?   Yes.   We have to talk soon."

Since music seemed to be giving Mike and I some clues into our relationship with songs of the past being played to each of us repeatedly, we listen carefully. Obviously, Mustang Sally was the first one.   There was a second one that I don't recall, but the third contained the words God speed my love.   There words were now being sung to me by Mike.

He was, in fact, serenading me in true sincerity, when I reacted with, "No, stop—" and put my hands up to indicate stay back.   We both laughed, because our love had come faster than the speed of light as it was, and so strongly.

Chapter Thirteen

Gut-Wrenching Love

The depth of my love is still growing, and it is being recognized and welcomed by Mike. It was Sunday morning, and we had awakened leisurely and were having coffee out on the patio in the sunshine.

"There is something that I must tell you," said Mike.

He then reached into his pocket and pulled out his wallet. He opened it to a picture he carried with him of a baby girl. "I don't know how else to tell you, but to show you. She's mine."

I was in total shock, but reacted as mildly as I could. My first thought was that this baby was an offspring from an affair, and I was trying to accept that, and what I was seeing was a reality.

"No, no, Mike corrected me." I then learned that this baby was from his last marriage, and had been conceived by a deliberate effort on his wife's part to save the troubled marriage.

I also learned that this had only added to the list of other manipulations in the marriage and had angered Mike enough to leave the marital home. A divorce resulted, and even though the process had been long, it had only been finalized probably less than two months ago.

Is this trouble for me, or what?

Where thoughts of perhaps a permanent relationship between Mike and myself had begun to creep in because of the depth of my feelings, I now knew that this could not be. We both, at this moment of truth, were wrenching in love and in agony, me because of what was true and in front of me, and he, feeling my pain.

The words of a rhyme which recently *came through me,* as Lillian claimed of the music she had written, replayed itself:

> Every thrill has its grief
> Every heartache its relief

I tried to accept this new information, but knew in my heart that I could never accept Mike into my life as a father of a three year old. I had been without children living at home for a number of years now.

He explained, of course, that he loved his baby, and I knew that this was true.

In trying to explain my feelings to him I stated, as delicately as I could, that there would always be a part of my heart that I would not be able to give him, because he could not give fully to me. He would always have part of his life with this little girl, and was responsible for her. He was not a free man. It was not as though his children were all grown, and we could concentrate on a life together, solely. He would have this commitment for many years of his life.

He painfully understood. He stated how he felt so relieved that he had finally told me. Right from the beginning, he had stated that he still had some issues to deal with, and that he would tell me at some time. He had already shared so much of his strife with me, I could hardly imagine what more he was harboring within. Now I knew, and the reality was confounding. It was restricting, confining, and confounding.

I responded that "What you feel in relief, has filled me with grief."

"I know," he said. "If you want to have me leave now, I will understand. I didn't want to tell you because I was afraid you would run. But I had to. You have to know."

His face and heart were filled with torture and fear. He awaited my reaction.

"I'm not going anywhere. I can't. I cannot accept this, but I'm not leaving. I have to think this through, so I'm going to reserve comment until I do."

Mike was satisfied and immensely relieved that I would just not tell him to leave my life. He looked as though his heart would virtually break, his emotions painfully displayed across his face. My pain, also, was cutting deeply within, but so was this love. He closed his wet eyes and took a deep breath when I assured him that I would not leave him.

I would not leave him now, but didn't know when I would. After all, I did not know why we were together or how long it was intended that this relationship last. I also felt that it was not in my control. It was predestined and prearranged, I was sure.

In an emotional conversation later in the day, I said dripping with love, "I know the depth of your passion; you don't even have to tell me."

He lost composure for a moment, embarrassed that I could see his exposed soul. I soothed him with a hug and a kiss. I didn't know what else I could do or say.

Chapter Fourteen

I Know Why

A quick call came in from Gwenn. She had just read another chapter in her book. "We have to talk," she said.

"Why?" I asked, wondering.

"Because I know why you and Mike are together."

"Why are we?" I couldn't wait to hear.

"You are brought together to have fun."

"That simple? There has to be more. There has to be another reason," I stated.

"Why?" she said. "Why can't that be it?"

"That hardly seems reason enough," I commented.

"You know that the couple in the book went to a channeler to find out why they were together, right? Well, they were brought together in this life to have fun. It seems that they had known each other in a previous life, in Greece, and had really enjoyed each other's company. They were not mates in that lifetime, but had agreed to come back to spend their lives together. It had been pre-arranged."

"Oh, so that's it." I exclaimed. "Do you really think that's why Mike and I are together?"

"You're having fun together, aren't you?" she asked.

"Yes, we are," I answered. "We certainly are."

"Well, maybe that's it, then. Just *sing in the sunshine and laugh in the rain*."

I left the conversation, still pondering these thoughts.

Just completing week four of the relationship, Mike and I had arranged to take off of work mid-week if the Red Wings won the championship. We would party into the night, and would be too tired to work the following day.

The Red Wings won the Stanley Cup, the second year in a row, and in keeping with our usual storybook affair, proceeded to have a marvelous time.

Mike had met me in the downtown area at a pub where my friend Kristen and I had planned to meet with our usual running and walking group. Kristen and I usually walked about four miles each week with the group. We were the walkers and not runners.

The crowd was primed, and we sat outdoors in front of a large-screened TV. Mike came equipped with party paraphernalia for the evening, which included a couple of brooms to celebrate the *clean sweep*! He also brought a stop sign indicating the party stops here, noise makers, streamers, and a homemade Stanley Cup. The cup consisted of a pitcher placed in a silver bag, with two outrageous winding and colorful straws from which we were to drink. He was clearly a showman, and reveled in the attention. He was also so glad to be accompanied by a mid-fiftyish party queen.

After the second period, we got into his car and drove across town to the west side to finish the celebration at one of his favorite spots that had dancing on a Tuesday night. We both loved music and dancing.

He had an ulterior motive, aside from liking the entertainment, and wanted to present me and show me off to his friends and recent girlfriends. He was truly proud, and continued to introduce me as the lady he had fallen in love with.

This introduction included the lady owner of the establishment, who was out on the dance floor with us. It was also a reaffirmation to his friend, Evan, whom I had met recently at another west-side dance establishment, and another male friend, Dave, with whom he had consummated male bonding.

He mused at the women in the place who had admired and dated him, and for whom he had no real interest. He had mentioned many times that they had pretty faces, but shared no chemistry with him. Even though I was miles and miles away, I was worth every millimeter! He was full of so much love. Actually, too much love.

Shall We Dance?

We danced until 2:30 a.m., leaving only to find a place to stay the night. He decided to drive back across town to the east side and cross the bridge to go to Windsor in Canada. I had not exactly planned to spend the night out; however, I must have somehow pre-planned the event by arranging to leave extra food out for the cat. I did not, however, pack clothing for an overnight stay or fresh clothes for the following day.

When Kristen asked if I had planned to stay overnight somewhere with him, I said no. I always had what I called an emergency repair kit in the car that included makeup, a toothbrush and hair spray, but I had not packed clothing. "So I slept in a towel," I remarked. "We had a toga party."

We arrived at our destination at 3:30 a.m. exhausted, so we both showered and fell asleep immediately. The morning brought beautiful sunshine, and we had breakfast in the hotel restaurant overlooking the river. Later, we strolled along the riverbank and into the Riverboat Casino to engage in some fun gambling with a moderate sum of money. This day did not provide winnings, but it did offer some entertainment.

Upon walking back to the hotel to check out, I explained Gwenn's findings from reading her book.

"I'll buy that," said Mike. "That's a good enough reason."

The afternoon brought lunch and hot-tubbing on the deck at my house followed by an afternoon nap. By late afternoon, around 4:30 p.m., Mike left to go to work and I left to meet some girlfriends for dinner.

Neither of us spoke about the three-year-old daughter and that of his spending the day with her on Tuesday, as he always did.

Chapter Fifteen

Keeping Score

In response to Gwenn's frequent inquiries of how things were going with Mike, I replied, "I think I'm dealing with a split soul, Gwenn. He's so much like Matt."

"Why not a transferred soul?" she asked.

"I don't know about that," I quickly retorted. "What is that?"

She laughed. "Or maybe it's a shared soul," she added. "Souls are not limited as we know humans to be. Maybe Matt's soul has transferred itself to Mike in order to complete a karma that would otherwise not be completed in this lifetime.

You know, you and Matt did not end your relationship with a peaceful resolution. That means the karma was not actually completed, and maybe you are to complete it with Mike. Maybe Matt's soul has temporarily transferred itself to Mike in order to do that. Maybe Mike will even feel a change if Matt's soul shares space in Mike's body to finish its karmic work."

"Now that's a scary thought," I said. "One of the first things Mike said to me was that he felt he was changing. I tried to give him some logical reasons why this might be, but I never thought of this."

She continued. "These are just concepts, now. Matt said to you, telepathically, that he would always be with you. It was as if to say, *if you need me, I will be there,* meaning the need to be with that soul, not person. Maybe he was really saying 'I will come to you in a way that you can't refuse me.'"

"Oh, I see. Because I would not welcome Matt back into my life peacefully, and would turn him away, you think he is coming to me in a way that cannot easily be recognized. Therefore I won't be able to refuse him."

"Yes. This way you can complete whatever karma it is that you were to complete, perhaps reach a peaceful resolution, but not actually be together."

"How strange a thought," I said. "Very perplexing."

"You already know that the similarities between Matt and Mike have gone far beyond coincidence. Why don't you try making a score sheet of all of the things in Mike's life that have an uncanny likeness to Matt's life?"

"That would be interesting," I said. "I'll try that."

Mike and Matt are both fair-skinned gentlemen, each having little to no body hair. Neither of them, I quickly recognized, ever had a mole removed from their body; it was not important to them, even though they both had egos. Thus far, Matt's looks were more important to him than Mike's; Mike's need is more for attention, and if he is thought to be funny.

70

Both Matt and Mike have two brothers. Matt has two sisters as well; Mike has none. Matt has three boys, Mike three girls, although his boy died at age 17. Note that Matt's youngest boy was four years old when I began seeing him; Mike's daughter is three. I was sixteen years younger then, so having a small child didn't have the same impact on me as it does now. Both men had a large age spread between the youngest child and older two.

The personalities of the two men are mysteriously similar. I have already stated that both have manic qualities, and I can predict Mike's every move because it mirrors the relationship I had with Matt.

I know Mike will call me several times throughout the day. I also know that I am on his mind constantly, within almost every thought. I also know that he will call me at the end of most every day. I can also count on a call shortly after his departure from my house, by cell phone, on his way home. The pattern is all so familiar, and comfortable, I might add, because that is what Matt did.

Neither Matt nor Mike are affluent. Both became financially encumbered later in life, but I feel that probably neither one of them handle money very well. At one point Matt's well went out, and he could not afford to have it fixed, thus no water. He was too proud to borrow the money, so he tried to exist without it for some time, showering at my place or his brother's.

71

I just learned that Mike is heavily burdened financially and is filing personal bankruptcy to rid himself of his recent and enormously expensive divorce. Neither gentleman seemed to mind spending money on our entertainment, though I find Mike to be watchful.

I met Matt at the company where we both worked. He was let go from that company without ever knowing the real cause. Being fired from a corporate job was quite uncommon. However, I do understand that one can be placed on a wrong track with the wrong people and there is no way to right the situation. It happens. After that I saw him through a couple more careers.

He first worked for a newly created division of an independent telephone company until the division closed. He had been offered a job by them to work in another state, but declined as he did not want to make the move. From there he landed a job with a pharmaceutical company and was able to also work into his day several personal endeavors of creative advertising and sell them effectively. He was successful at creating his own business and marketed it well for several years.

Now for Mike's background. Mike is in sales for a major phone concern selling cable television. He is going door-to-door, calling on families at their homes. It isn't much of a career for a man of his age, but the pay is adequate , especially for the minimal time he puts in per week. The job is pretty much stress free and fits his type of personality. Rejection in sales can only be handled by a certain few, I find, and despite the nongrowth type of job that it is, his ego is flattered by earning the title of number one salesman. He is always getting accolades, prizes and perks. His management and peers recognize him as an accomplished salesperson.

At the time that I met Mike, he told me that the company that he had worked for had been bought out by another concern. He told me that he has been in several high-level positions with large ad agencies, and is really more of a marketing and promotion person. Ad jobs, I know, are quick to end by being fired, so it was no surprise when he told me that he had been fired on one occasion. Other incidences happened along the way, like companies bringing in their own management, or some just closing down. I understood that all of these things do happen.

I have observed that he has an identical talent for selling as Matt, however he is more aggressive in nature. Matt is more smooth and disarming, and is slower to close the sale. Both know how to work smart, and are confident of their abilities. Against the direction of their employers, they both short-cut their work efforts, and save hours of work in the field for excellent results. They are paid for their talent rather than their time.

Both Mike and Matt brought me gifts from points earned from sales, with no money exchanging hands. In fact, both of them found reason to give me a small figurine of Minnie Mouse during one point in the relationship.

This makes me feel as if God is sending me all the possible clues to recognize that I am dealing with the same soul. Mike's daughter works for a pharmaceutical company. Mike's daughter's boyfriend is an advertising and marketing man. Mike's landlord is a pharmacist. Mike's closest male friend is a psychiatrist.

Did Matt not deal with psychotropics in his career and take me to mingle with his doctor acquaintances, attend psychiatrist's talks and pharmacist's conventions?

Again, it's like the song Mustang Sally, with Ride Sally Ride, and God saying, "Did you get it?"

"Yes, God, I think so. What is it that I am supposed to do?"

Chapter Sixteen

Storybook Life

I had felt that my life was as happy and fulfilling as a storybook life for some time, as I needed nothing or no one to be complete. It felt perfect. I had my two grown children who were loving and cared about me, and some very good friends that I could count on. I was totally whole by myself, and happy with what I had.

That does not mean that I wasn't willing to welcome a gentleman into my life. After all, I believe that most women who are alone actually go through life wishing to meet a wonderful person to share their life with. Few, if any, are truly happy to go through life alone, even if they don't admit it.

I hope to convey that the incidents that happen in my life are noteworthy on a spiritual level. That is why I write about them. The documentation of what I feel is happening with me and my soul mates may pertain to my readers, as well as others, on a universal level. It has to do with having all of the pieces of a huge puzzle fall into place, perfectly timed, in order to complete our missions here on earth. By soul mates, I mean all those who travel through this lifetime, and probably other lifetimes, with me.

Here I am, with a man who has the most endearing qualities, and there seem to be insurmountable impediments before me. The three-year-old child seems to be the real crux, as this is something I really don't want in my life. I resent not being able to be this man's main importance, even knowing that children always come first in a relationship. Others might overcome this hurdle more easily, but I don't feel that it is right for me. I do feel, however, that our meeting was for the purpose of completing some karma—whatever that might be, and it may be a message to me regarding the small child.

Therefore, I plan to continue enjoying Mike's loving nature and friendship. I admitted to him this morning that I acknowledged the fact that he had a small daughter, even if I had not accepted it. I was, in fact, ignoring it at this time.

Inwardly I have withdrawn a great deal of my feelings. I have put them in a vault, so to speak. But, as Gwenn points out to me, I should just continue to *sing in the sunshine and laugh in the rain* with him. I don't think he is aware of my partial withdrawal.

So many times he looks at me and says, "You look like you're 16 years old." Somewhat flattered, I would smile and think to myself, *are you seeing me from a previous life?*

I have heard that sometimes one can look at someone's face and suddenly look beyond and see another face in their place. The new face is actually another face of a previous lifetime attached to the same soul.

Then one day, we were enjoying ourselves in the outdoor hot tub on my deck, and the sun was shining in his face. This time I saw the little boy in him. It was so distracting that I could not think of anything except the little boy that I was seeing. He looked about nine years old.

I've since seen that young boys' face again, and now when he says, "You look like you're about 16 years old," I think yes, I see the little boy in you, too.

I wonder if we were adoring brother and sister in a former life. He sometimes comments on how we adore each other now. To have us each look back and see a young child tells me that it must have been a pleasant period in our lifetime together.

Chapter Seventeen

An Encounter with Purpose

Gwenn tells me that she has finished reading the book that dealt with the relationship that modeled mine with Mike. She has told me that the two did not consummate their relationship; they still had love for one another, but were now friends and not lovers.

"Why is that?" I asked. "What broke them apart?"

"Basically, they agreed that he was too Russian and she too American."

"That's it?" I asked.

"Yes, that was it. They apparently completed whatever they were to complete together, and they remain friends."

Reflecting back on the couple, "How long were they together?" I asked.

"For a year and a half."

So, will Mike and I be together for a fast and furious year and a half? Is that what I am supposed to do? I wondered.

"Are you ready for some new assignments?" asked Gwenn.

"Like what," I was curiously awaiting her direction.

"This is to see if you really are dealing with the same soul. Try sending a message to Mike telepathically. See if you can get an answer."

"Oh, like I did with Matt?"

"Yes."

"Okay."

"Then, sometime later, after you have completed this, try sending a message to Matt. See if he is still *home*. Then maybe you will know where Matt's soul is. You will have to try to select something in your message that is exclusive to Matt and could not be confused with Mike. Maybe something about Matt's sister, since Mike doesn't have one. You'd better verify that, though."

"Very interesting thoughts. How do you come up with this stuff?"

"Here's another one for you," she continued. "Note anything that Mike comes up with that is particularly unique, maybe something he says. That might tie a time period or place as to when you were together before. The man in the book I've read always said, 'Bless you. Have a good night's sleep.' They were somehow able to tie that back to a past life wherein he used the same words."

"Okay," I said, still wallowing in my thoughts.

"That goes for you, too. There may be something that you say to Mike that could be considered a unique statement."

"I'll think about it, and watch for it," I agreed.

Chapter Eighteen

Karmic Work to Complete

I'm starting to understand that there is a definite purpose or karmic feat taking place in my relationship with Mike. I told him that I was beginning to see that he had some karmic work to do, and I would share it with him when I had it sorted out and understood it myself.

He acknowledged my need to sort it out first, but was concerned that it was going to affect our relationship. He was afraid that I was going to address not seeing one another, or some other monumental problem.

I assured him that I was not. I knew that I was going to be a part of this endeavor; I only hoped that I would understand what it was that I was to complete, and what I needed to learn by this experience.

Matt spent so much time with me, that he neglected the needs of his children. When he would spend time with me, he would feel guilty that he was not at home with his family, especially the youngest boy. When he would spend time at home, he would feel guilty that he was not with me. The burden became too large, and the pull on each end so great, that he asked to take an intermission from the relationship. His older boys had let him know in their own way that what he was doing, they understood, was right for him, but it was not right for them. Matt had family debts to pay, and our relationship ultimately ended.

Now I have met Mike. He has three girls. His oldest is out of state and does not speak to him. She is very angry, but at this time I do not have the whole story. His second daughter and he have a wonderful, loving relationship.

Mike has told me that his daughter has agreed that he has made some mistakes. She forgives him, and loves him very much. That was quite obvious to me in our meeting one another. His youngest, now three, is seemingly very loving to him.

I somehow feel that the karmic lesson has something to do with balancing the relationship with me and the responsibility of his children. While Matt refused to have me as part of his family life, he was very much a part of mine with my children. Mike may have a similar challenge in making the balance work.

And, most certainly, Mike must make amends with his oldest daughter before his karmic work is done. The challenges ahead are mind boggling, and yet I don't feel I am to be a permanent part. Where am I to fit? What is it that I should do? Am I a guide? A catalyst? The balance? The thing that makes it all work? Could it possibly be that Mike's challenge is to make us all happy, and for us all to accept one another? Is my direction to stay with him and live in harmony?

If so, I would have a tremendous, formidable task ahead of me, and one that I am not sure I am willing to take on.

What is Mike to do? Where does he begin? At what point will he find that carrying me in his life is inhibiting the relationship with one or more of his children? How far down the line will he need to make the break to complete his karmic work? What choices will he need to make?

About all of these things, I wonder.

Chapter Nineteen

Time Seems to be Irrelevant

It has been a couple of months, now, that I have known Mike and have enjoyed his continuing companionship. A more rational pattern has been established that allows us to see one another but get much needed sleep. He does not stay over on Sunday night and get up at 5:00 a.m. with me, and I do not attempt to meet him after he gets out of work at 8:30 or 9:00 and stay up late to meet him. Working opposite shifts has brought extraordinary challenges for us.

For the first two months of our relationship, it was unusual that Mike was assigned sales territories on the east side of town where he would be closer to me. That meant that I could be more accessible and we could find a convenient place to meet.

However, the last two weeks he has been assigned a territory that is more than an hour away, so driving to meet me and then another hour to get home just didn't make any sense at all. Fortunately, God was kind enough to see that we had spent ample time together in the beginning in order to adjust to this new schedule. We felt that we could now stay apart for more than a twenty-four hour period.

What was this draw, anyway? I'm still stunned about our dual reaction of instantaneous love and attraction. Just as curious is the pace at which this relationship is traveling. We are as comfortable as if we had spent eons of time together.

We have now successfully been apart all week for two weeks now, not meeting until Friday night. In some ways it was a good break for me. I needed to catch up with myself and pay attention to friendships I had not had time for.

Mike, on the other hand, claims, "You were fine with this, but I wasn't. I still missed you terribly. I know that your life is a lot fuller than mine, and you keep a lot busier. I know your life is healthier because you have so many interests. I need to work on that."

Spending time at the gambling casino in Windsor was not the right answer, but that is how Mike decided to spend his free time away from me. When I learned of this, it really concerned me. He had just had a company-paid vacation in Las Vegas before we met, and had won about $3,500.

Since that winning, he and I went to the Windsor casino three times, not playing more than $20.00 at a time. Now he tells me that he has been back, playing larger stakes. He won $2,300 on one visit, which he told me about. On a subsequent day, he lost it all, and then proceeded to win it back, plus more. The end result was a positive $3,200.

What I didn't know was that Mike had awakened at 5:00 a.m. that morning and had gone to the Casino. Since he works late into the evening, he is a late sleeper. It is not normal for him to get up at 5:00 a.m. Now, even he was concerned. The rush he felt from winning was frightening. Even the cash winnings were bothering him. He spent an entire hour with a therapist working on what seemed to be a forming addiction.

When I learned the whole story, I was grateful that he became concerned and had addressed it. How can such a good person have so much bad karma? He can be so easily dissuaded and continues to follow wrong paths. I can only hope that he learns from his mistakes.

Chapter Twenty

Indianapolis

We may have been able to adapt to seeing each other only on weekends when our schedules forced it, but I didn't mention that in the short time we've known each other, we have managed to take three vacations.

I'm including a one-night stay in Windsor when the Red Wings won the Stanley Cup, followed by a nine-day straight stay at my house while I had my bathroom remodeled.

Our third vacation was a four-day weekend, when Mike won a trip to Indianapolis for the Brickyard 400. He said he wasn't into racing, but would enjoy the party atmosphere. He didn't know that I had incurred some auto racing in my background. I had worked on the Corvette program for some time, and would actually enjoy it.

Isn't this a romantic, storybook love affair I'm living?

Every day at Indy was fun packed. Thursday was a travel day, starting with lunch at a west side deli on his side of town. He had hoped to make a reservation at a resort-like Inn at a state park in Indianapolis for our return trip, but there were no vacancies available.

We got into Indianapolis, checked in, and went to dinner at a place called Rock Bottom. Later we went to Ike and

Jones for dancing and had a great time. It reminded me of the kind of places I had been to in Chicago when I was seeing Matt.

Friday was race day at the track, but not the 400. This race was scheduled from 1:30 to 3:30, so we planned to have lunch in the suite provided by his company and watch the race. Lunch began with Bloody Marys. He also had pit passes, of no interest to him, but he was kind enough to get them for our use because of my interest.

"Can't you feel the thunder?" I wailed as we proceeded down to the pits. The roar of the engines and speed of the cars on the track whirred in the air. I was exhilarated! He pacified me. I made him endure a half-hour or so in the intense heat, and he managed to accommodate me.

My enthusiasm amused him, and my racing outfit captivated him. I had worn a white top and slacks with a sporty red, white and black lightweight jacket. That, with checkered sunglasses and a red hat to shield the sun made him very proud to have me join his company members.

Mike said we started out at Rock Bottom and then ended up in the pits. It could only get better from there!

We went back to the hotel and got cleaned up for the evening. We put our name in for a reservation at an Italian restaurant which had a two-hour wait, and then walked the four-story mall for an hour. We stopped for a Spanish Coffee, which was called a Mexican Coffee in Indy, at an outdoor cafe. There were so many places to go there. We intended to go out after dinner, but were too tired. Five minutes of TV and we were both asleep.

On Saturday we went to the pool in the morning, and then to Champps for lunch. Champps was a favorite hangout for him when he lived in Indianapolis a short time ago, and he was pleased to take me there. The place was huge, with two bars separated by a long, charming outdoor path and benches along the way.

It was also a great place to watch the Brickyard 400 on a big screen TV which was taking place that day. We then went to Dick Clark's American Bandstand, with all the decor of the old bandstand. It had the original contracts of the early performers like Elvis, with a compensation of $450.00, which was crossed out with a replacement figure of $150.00.

That evening we headed back to that beautiful State Park with the Inn, but there were still no vacancies. We stayed at a nearby motel and paid double, I'm sure, for a nice room that had a Jacuzzi. That evening, we went back to the park for an outdoor concert.

We returned to the State Park on Sunday to enjoy the lake and had brunch at the Inn. We felt so overstuffed from the whole trip, and started for home around 4:00 p.m. On the way home, we stopped at a roadside stand and bought fresh sweet corn, green beans and tomatoes to make dinner that night.

What a fun time we had! We are able to spend endless
hours together quite comfortably.

Chapter Twenty-One

The Same Soul

We still had not addressed any issues of karmic work to be done, or talked about what reasons might be at the forefront of our acquaintance. We have merely enjoyed the relationship, and perhaps been concerned with its shortcomings on both our parts.

Although we have discussed relatively little, I did tell Mike that I knew that he was looking for someone to take care of him, and that wouldn't work for me. I had the same goal of finding someone who wanted to take care of me.

Gwenn corrected me to say, "You don't want someone to take care of you. You want someone to pamper you. I can't imagine you letting anyone take care of or control you. That wouldn't last at all."

"I guess you're right," I said. "I do have the tendency to control. Mike recognizes that as well, and he seems to be attracted to those who take care of and control him. He also knows that is not good for him. I do both, but I object to not feeling like I'm the one being taken care of."

"A balance is what is needed," Mike said. "It should be a balance."

While Mike's comfortable manner and charm surround me, I am still in awe at the replication I feel in the two personalities of Matt and Mike.

"Look for a sign, perhaps a phrase or something said by Mike to find the place and time that the two of you have lived before," said Gwenn.

Well, curiously enough, a statement made by Matt is now being made by Mike. Why is this personality so repetitious in its needs and in its behavior?

Mike would ask me, "Did you put that on for me?" Or, "Did you buy that to wear for me?"

When I replied honestly that I actually did not, the response was exactly the same as Matt's.

"Can't you just lie to me? Can't you just say that you did?"

Chapter Twenty-Two

His Smiling Face

It is late August, and Mike and I have been seeing each other for three months now. It feels like years due to our comfort level. We are allowing our feelings to become established and grow, almost denying what is developing before us at a breakneck speed.

I know that I have issues to deal with in this relationship, and in fairness to him need to bring them out into the open. They are weighing so heavy on me, and yet I don't want to place another hurdle in front of us. On the other hand, who is to say that he is ready to confirm that kind of commitment anyway?

Commitment? No, this love is for the here and now, even though I allow definite thoughts drift in a more permanent direction. I know in my heart that this is not an ever-lasting love. It is to take care of whatever purpose it is intended to complete, and then for us each to go on our separate ways.

You might call this gut feel, or common sense. You might call it reality.

I have previously been accused of having conditional love. I strenuously objected to the accusation from Matt when he first brought up the subject. I didn't agree that my love for him was at all conditional. I loved him completely. But, in fact, it was and is conditional with

Mike. Perhaps it is because I know more of what it is that I want, and have higher expectations of someone to meet my needs.

Life's needs seem to be cumulative. Did you ever consider that? I want the caring nature and security offered by my former husband. I loved the way he would just naturally take care of making the decisions I found difficult, the way he mended my open wounds, and made all of my little wants into granted wishes with natural ease. It was too bad that he didn't take care of his health or his weight.

I also want the handsome body and warm and charming personality of Matt, who also held me in high esteem and on a pedestal. He, too, was capable of helping me make those complicated decisions, and fix those things that needed to be taken care of in a home. And, of course, I want a man who can model the great lover that he was.

Lastly, although extreme good looks should not be a requirement, I want to feel as good as I felt accompanied by a man as handsome as Steve who also adored me. Although Mike is quite handsome, in my mad attraction for him there is something missing in the chemical equation, and I want it all!

I read my horoscope for the week with intrigue, written by Brady, my favorite writer. While most predictions are skillfully ambiguous, this one appeared to be straightforward and to the point. It stated unequivocally that Capricorns would be the wealthiest, most intelligent, and most handsome in his or her lifetime AND be paired with a gorgeous person of the opposite sex who would also be the most intelligent and wealthy of his or her lifetime—THIS WEEK. It stated that this would fit most Capricorns. Mike and I are both Capricorns.

Wouldn't that be a grandiose and fortunate event? It's something to dream on, anyway.

I repeated this prediction to Gwenn. She said that she wished that it was her horoscope. Gwenn's former husband is also a Capricorn, sharing the same birthday as Mike.

"I wish it would be true," I said, "but you know how doubtful that is, even though I believe Brady is right most of the time. It's just too good to be true. It sounds like a perfect solution to my mounting predicament with Mike. I love him, but something is telling me that it just isn't right."

Another person introduced might prove to be a distraction for either one of us, or an impediment forming a triangle. I have seen Mike's roving eye, and his flirtatious nature in the works. I can tell when he has been admired by another woman or is attracted to their personality. Although there are countless good things to be certain, this relationship is not rock solid. Are any of them, I ask?

It is Saturday night, and Mike and I are going out for the evening. We are very much aware that our love is growing, but I am mindful that it is probably not a perfect love or an all-consuming love on either part. I just can't put my finger on what it is that is missing. We always have a good time and enjoy each other's company immensely.

We headed west, but were still on the east side on the main highway that I take every day to go to work. Mike affectionately held my hand in the car while driving along. We were engaged in conversation, and I wore a smile upon my face. I glanced at the car in the lane next to me while we were paused at the light. A very handsome man was smiling back at me. This was more than just a casual smile. His expression was beaming with delight, and he was smiling back at me. I did not recognize him as anyone that I might know.

We pulled ahead in traffic as the light changed. I again glanced over to find this gorgeous, well-defined face still smiling at me. Mike was unaware of what was going on, and I did not mention it to him. I did find it to be a mysterious encounter, however. The Brady horoscope passed through my mind. Was this the man that I was to be paired with this week?

Only my life would have such a cosmic occurrence, I thought, for it was only I who picked up so many clues of the master plan that was being presented before me. One must always be aware, I thought. I did not deny any obscure or remote feelings or let thoughts escape the realm of potential reality.

Then I wondered what plane I was on in this little understood spherical place, and where I stood in completing my karma.

Of course I knew that if it was the man predicted in my horoscope, that our actual meeting would have to take place at a later time. Only our faces had met. We had made eye contact, and the acknowledgement was there. Why did I feel such confidence that I would meet this man in person some day, with this being such a bizarre matter?

I considered that this line of thinking was absurd, but the feeling was that this is the man I am to be paired with. Might this be another prospect I am to encounter in this lifetime? Perhaps he is my final mate. Wouldn't that be wonderful if it indeed were to happen and be right?

He was out of view now, and although I was discretely trying to find his car in my line of sight via the rearview mirror, he was gone.

My thoughts wandered. I tried to recollect where I might have seen this face before. A resurgence of a business trip taken many years ago crossed my mind. I was at an airport in Pennsylvania awaiting my connecting flight to one of the automotive plant cities. A big storm came through and knocked out all of the power.

People were using their Bic cigarette lighters when needing to use the restroom because the entire airport was dark except for the daylight coming in the window.

A nice looking gentleman in the airport, also waiting for his next flight, had taken notice of me. He offered me some pretzels from an opened bag in his hand. I had been reading a book, but was aware that he had been watching me while he was walking around.

He was a well-seasoned traveler, and knew that with all electricity out that planes would continue to fly in, but none could leave. He kept checking with the gal at the desk to see if the power was being restored. "They are still having difficulty," she reported.

I was unaware that all fueling equipment was electronic, and without electricity no planes could refuel. That meant that all passengers, those still coming in and those intending to leave would be stranded in this city looking for a room if the problem was not corrected.

The gentleman checked the counter again to get a status of the problem, and came back to me to report that all auxiliary power systems were out also. It could be hours before electricity was restored.

Chances are it would not be restored anytime soon, as the storm was severe and had reached across several miles.

The man who was favoring me paced a little longer, and then clued me in to a probable scenario that would happen in and around the airport. He suggested that I catch a cab with him and get out of the immediate city limits. I did, which was a wise choice. The power was off in all of the local hotels that we passed, and people were standing outside in front of the hotels because there was no air conditioning inside.

With this man's assistance, I stayed in a comfortable, air-conditioned room for the night after enjoying his company, dinner and some dancing. His personality was so easy to become close to, and had he been local I would definitely have been interested in him.

We met in the morning for breakfast, and then made our departures to our separate locations without ever a contact again. Of all of the pleasantries of this encounter, I never did forget his nice smile.

I now wonder in which lifetime we may have met, and if so, what part of life did we at some time share.

His face reminded me of the smiling man in the car next to me, but it was not him. *This smiling face belonged to the man I didn't know I have always been waiting to meet.* His smile was so intent on me.

While riding along, I caught a glimpse of his profile with a broadened smile, as he looked straight ahead while driving. The cheek structure was oh, so familiar; it was a rounded apple cheek that I most certainly loved. His face was so alluring, I knew it was the face of the man I was to love. This man was to love me also, and he knew it. He was looking at me as if to say, *"There she is. I have found her."*

He was wonderful! I knew it. It would be wonderful!

I reported this strange and obscure incident to Gwenn during a phone conversation.

"That's it. There's your man in the horoscope. You have met him. You will meet him again. He will show up somewhere. What kind of car did he drive? What was his license plate?"

She knew that I often read them for meanings.

"I don't know. I couldn't see the car or the plate. I could only see the front fender and door. It was a pale gray, almost white. That's all I could see."

In retrospect, I now realize how rare the color was on his car. It was not a standard color for any classic car of today. It must be a more prestigious car, perhaps one that not everyone can afford. It had a squared rather than rounded front fender. Perhaps it was a Lexus.

I had noticed this man near the Lexus dealer, which was located on that main road, but it was Saturday, and the dealership was not even open.

"Gwenn! Now why would a man look into the car at me while I'm riding with another man? What reason would he have to look at me and smile like that?"

"None, unless he was your soul mate. You have lived thousands of years and have many soul mates."

"Why are they all coming at me in this lifetime at this particular time?" I asked. "In just the last three years I have loved Matt, Steve, and now Mike."

"Who knows. I guess it's your time to meet them. Enjoy it."

"I'm still enjoying Mike," I countered.

"That's why this was only a first meeting of the eyes," said Gwenn. "If it is time for this man to enter your life, you will leave Mike. Maybe your work with Mike will be done shortly. Whatever love you have for him will have served its purpose. You will move on."

"It's nice to know that you understand that I do have love for Mike but feel it is not forever. And, I knew you were the only one I could tell about this smiling man and you would understand what it was all about."

"Oh yes. I understand, all right. Mike might be very worth loving, but he is not what you want."

Chapter Twenty-Three

The Gods will Decide

I've never been known to be a dreamer; reality is where I've always lived. I might have looked upon card readings as entertainment or intrigue, or specific happenings as omens, but I was pretty solid in my closed-in world.

In more recent years, I have opened up to the abilities of physic readers and other known phenomena. It is little wonder, then, that my daughter brought me a Genie bottle from a flea market when she recently visited her father in Florida. She also brought me a small amount of witches oil that she got from our friend, Brenda, the Tarot card reader and former neighbor.

While I don't really believe in its myth at this point in my life, I ceremoniously placed the oil in the bottle, and extracted a small amount to place on my wrist as I had been instructed. Then I made my wish.

As the same point in time, Brady had made his prediction of Capricorns being paired with their most perfect mates. The fact that I was teased this week by an on-looking man, of whom I presume would satisfy the requirement, life again awaits all things to be in place before an action is completed. The Gods will decide if and when. I use the term Gods to mean God and his loyal angelic helpers.

In fact, when asking God if I would be meeting up with Steve again in my life, or if Steve would be a mate for me, I got nebulous answers. I was left with: The Gods have not decided. Because of the indecisive answer, I also understood that the matter was under consideration.

I was actually visited twice by the angels in regard to my asking about Steve. When I awakened in the morning, I could feel their presence, which is an extreme rarity, but real. I cannot create this feeling. I could not create this feeling again when they were gone.

Meanwhile, in this very loving relationship with Mike, I am more definite in feeling that I don't want this to be permanent. I don't know how to tell him, however, and I certainly would hate to spoil what we are both enjoying so well.

As I look back, this may be exactly how Matt felt about his relationship with me. He kept saying that he needed to take an intermission from me, but just couldn't do it. He enjoyed our time together so well that it was difficult to leave. Now I am faced with this same reality with Mike. This might indeed be the biggest reason that Matt has intruded upon Mike by sharing space with his soul. Perhaps he wanted me to know just how he felt.

Just as Matt felt about his relationship with me, I'm also looking forward to the many plans that Mike and I have made, as I know how dearly we enjoy our time together. I'm sure that the matter will be addressed in due time, at some very painful point in our courtship.

My thoughts always target on his having an infant daughter who resides with his former wife, but there are other issues that are now making me uncomfortable. The most important of these is that he has no interest in having a home. He seems unable or unwilling to do or help with the most common chores in maintaining a home.

I fear he is also at a loss to take care of himself in day-to-day living. He not only is unknowing of how to do these things, he doesn't want to know. He doesn't want to take care of a house and wants to be a maintenance-free man. In fact, he wants someone to take care of him. He needs someone to take care of him.

At one point, Kristen asked me if I had met Mike's youngest daughter yet. I said "No, I haven't."

"And, you don't want to, do you!" she postulated.

"No, I don't. I don't want this to be part of my life."

While I feel somewhat guilty in my awareness of these matters, I really feel that Mike needs me in his life at this time. His life continues to be plagued with taking care of major obstacles that he has created for himself. They need to be addressed one by one, because of their magnitude, and having me in his life allows a nice cushion for him to lean on.

At present, these include personal bankruptcy and back taxes owed to the Internal Revenue for the last few years. I know that my existence in his life gives him great pleasure, and I do give him love—just not everlasting love.

Lillian, too, questions my continuance of the relationship knowing how I feel. "Well, it must feel right," she said, "or you wouldn't be in the relationship."

"Yes," I agreed, "it does feel right."

"Then that's what you should go on," she stated. "It has to feel right."

Might it be that I will end up with Mike by default? And might it be that we can work out these thorny issues? He is truly so loving and caring.

Soon after Kristen made her comment to me, Mike stated that I would be meeting his little daughter some time soon.

Chapter Twenty-Four

Life is a Vacation

It is now four months into the relationship, and a fourth mini-vacation is to take place. It has been wonderful for me, and I so look forward to time with this man. It is such a necessary fulfillment for me. I long for the opportunity to be with him without the interruption of everyday living.

"You like to travel, don't you," Mike said, more of a statement than a question.

"No, I don't. I just love the time away with you," I answered.

When each weekend rolls around, the pressures of the upkeep of the house, the chores undone, and the weeds overgrown become overwhelming. All I have done since I met Mike is enjoy him and the time we spend together.

As I have said, Mike is certainly not at all interested in doing anything that resembles work around the house. Under duress, he will pleasantly assist me, but I know it is never on his agenda. He is clearly not a homemaker in any way.

A planner and party-maker he is, and he's wonderful at it. Being a marketing man, he looks for every opportunity to have fun and to make the most of it. It's a great life if you don't have any responsibilities.

His entire spare time, if not checking out the entertainment section of the newspaper, is spent watching some kind of sport on television, either at home or at a pub. To his credit, he keeps contact with some male friends, but since each seem to have as much idle time as Mike, I suspect they are drifters as well. One of his friends is an established psychiatrist, but since he has ample time to hang out, he is probably an apartment dweller as well and has no responsibility.

I can make allowances for Mike as he has many serious issues to deal with at this time. I would agree that a no-stress job and no-stress life is probably what he needs. He had just gone through a divorce right before I met him, leaving a three-year old daughter behind. That is enough pressure for anyone.

Added to this, the debts incurred by the divorce lead him into personal bankruptcy. That was the second *big* news that he dropped on me, ever so carefully. He knew that it would impact the relationship as well.

This weekend we are attending a college football game in Ann Arbor. Because Mike does not move fast in the morning, and the game starts at noon, he has thoughtfully made room reservations for us at a motel nearby. That way we can awaken leisurely, have a light breakfast, and make our way to the game.

It was a beautiful sunny day, and warm as well. I had not expected the temperature to climb to such heights, so

I had not packed any short-sleeved shirts. One would assume a football game would call for some cool weather, but it was bordering on hot. We stopped at a Meijer's store on the way, and I picked up a Spartan green shirt to wear with my new Spartan hat that Mike had thoughtfully bought for me.

It didn't matter what we did or where we went, we were totally comfortable together. We were alike in our temperaments, needs, and desires. We were hungry at the same time, felt like walking at the same time, and got tired at the same time.

While we had intended to stay for the nightlife in Ann Arbor after the game, we both became so sleepy that we decided to just drive home. We stopped for a cold pop on our way, and went back to his place to take a nap.

That evening brought more fun and dancing, as Mike always sought out live music and dancing every weekend.

I had wanted to get home to take care of some of the unfinished work at my house, but Mike suggested we take a nice walk in the nature trail by his place the next morning. That sounded too appealing to pass up. The wonderful weather would soon be gone, so now was the time to enjoy it.

I stayed the night, and we had coffee outside on his deck in the morning, and later went for that wonderful walk. This trail had been touted to be the best nature trail in the county, and I could see why. We passed two very private lakes with a couple of beautiful homes and lovely trees around them, and then crossed a main road with gorgeous, larger lakes on either side.

It was so picturesque, maybe even more than my lake at home. My lake was much larger, and when there was humidity in the air, you lost sight of the string of islands on the other side.

Continuing our walk, at the point where we met the main highway, there were a few restaurants and a coffee house. On our return, we stopped and had a salad for lunch before continuing our journey back.

It was then time to start off for home, with little time left to do the many things that I needed to do.

Chapter Twenty-Five

Depression Hits

For the second time this week, while at work, I found myself suddenly faced with depression. I have no idea why, and haven't suffered from depression for many years.

My usual solution was to see if I was carrying a lot of water in my system, as this would sometimes set me off in that direction. I could usually tell by checking my stomach to see if it was extended, but this didn't seem to be the case. I had no idea where this feeling of despair was coming from.

Nothing at work was bothering me. Nothing at home was bothering me. And it wasn't a severe depression, just dips of gloom for no apparent reason. The depression would wave in and out, but would stay for considerably longer periods than I was comfortable with.

Mike asked if he had done anything to cause the depression.

"No," I said. "I don't know what it's from." And I didn't. There was no reason that I knew.

On the weekends I was fine again. Mike would pack his clothes and stay at my house, mostly because he lived such a distance from me. I sometimes wished I had some weekend time alone , but he carefully stayed out of my way and we lived comfortably under one roof. I was able to take time to do washing and clean house, and he would either watch a game on television or take his newspaper and coffee and go sit on the deck by the lake.

That would allow me to move about the house freely, talk to my friends on the phone, and generally do what I needed to do. Mike would leave either Saturday or Sunday to work for a few hours.

One Saturday, when I was planning to wallpaper the bathroom, he asked if I minded if he went to listen to a lecture at church. Of course, I didn't mind. I was glad he had somewhere to go. I didn't need his help to wallpaper, and he was grateful!

When I returned to work, the depression again began to drift into my life. I still questioned what was causing it. Why was this happening? I knew it wasn't the job.

I began to wonder if it was something about having Mike in my life that was bothering me. He was a wonderful planner of entertainment, and we were still having a lot of fun. Maybe it was some weekend privacy that I needed. Maybe it was the fact that Mike's life was not the match for me. Maybe the added pressures of Mike's serious dilemmas were piling up and affecting me. No, no, I thought. That really wasn't it.

I learned that Mike not only had a personal bankruptcy to contend with, he now was facing the fact that he had evaded filing taxes for about ten years. Feeling like a fugitive, just one step ahead of the IRS, he was now contacting tax accountants to assist him in addressing the issue.

This was an added pressure that I felt, but I didn't feel it was the cause of my depression. Mike had told me that he had paid taxes every year through his payroll deductions, as the companies he worked for withdrew the funds automatically. He just hadn't filed. He had no idea what his debt and penalty would be, but, he was now ready to address this and was feeling better about himself.

He confessed that the IRS had finally contacted him. He knew that they would catch up with him before long. For years he had moved from state to state with his jobs and had not been traced. He was living back in Michigan for the second year in a row, and Uncle Sam had found him. Now he had to contact his best choice of tax accountants and respond to the situation, which he did expediently. I would not want to live like that!

To add to his grief, Mike now admits to having a gambling addiction. When he felt he was out of control, he sought help from his therapist to work through the problem.

With each added problem, my heart would ache more. This I did not need. This was a major hurdle to living with Mike in my life.

Now I knew there were too many things to make allowances for, too many things to excuse in the relationship. It could never work. I could never feel comfortable. I would always be ill at ease, never knowing when the next emotional blow would hit. Never knowing when the next big disappointment would strike.

I still felt it was his problem, not mine, but I knew now that I had to face telling Mike that he and I can never be.

At my lowest point of my very mild depression, I decided that I would talk to Mike. But when I would begin, he was so uplifting that my spirits would soar and I would be fine again. He could bring me out of any slump. I just couldn't quite put my finger on why I was slumping.

I now recall that the last time I felt depression like this was at the realization that I was unhappy with my marriage. It ultimately ended in divorce. That should tell me something.

I discussed this perplexing situation with my daughter one evening when she stopped by. I told her of how depressed I had been, and how I suspected that it was due to the relationship I had with Mike.

To my surprise, she understood completely and agreed that it probably was. She told me how she had felt when she was in a relationship with a going nowhere man, and how it satisfied her and depressed her at the same time.

"I think you're just not proud of him, Mom," she said. "He doesn't match what you're all about."

"What do you mean?" I asked.

"Well, his life isn't going anywhere. He's ringing doorbells for a living. He isn't excelling in anything."

I agreed. "He's got so much going on in his life, I think that's all he can handle right now," I said. "But you're right. He probably doesn't have the ambition to do much else with his life. He has no real goals for himself."

"And that's not what you're all about," she continued. "Look at you. You started out as a file clerk and now you're an engineer. Someone like Mike is not going to make you happy. I might be old fashioned, but the man should be the breadwinner. He should be working at making a lot of money for you and for your security."

"You might be right. That might be part of what is bothering me."

I thought it over for a few days, and began to feel sure that the same man who could delight me and make me happy, could also make me blue. Now I had to rationalize what the real issues were so that I could thoughtfully and carefully relate them to him.

That would not be easy. Every thought that I assembled in my mind to begin such a discussion quickly turned to rage. I would conjure some very hurtful statements in my mind, and I did not want to do this. He did not deserve this treatment. I really loved him; he just was not one I could settle for.

I had to figure something out. I was loving all of the fun things that we did, but I could only contain this building rage for so long. And it was building. Every time I thought about explaining myself, small things would build to explosive levels. How could I even begin to tell him what I was feeling?

Chapter Twenty-Six

How Can I Tell Him?

I told my friends Kristen and Mary about the situation in which I have found myself. They both agree that the realization of a relationship that is not going anywhere can cause depression.

I know that I must tell him, and whatever I say will hurt him. I also know that it will hurt me. I enjoy his companionship, his humor and laughter so much that this will not be easy. The more I deliberate on this task, the more I know it is the right thing to do.

I am biding my time. I want to carefully think through what the things are that are bothering me most, the things that would absolutely not allow the relationship to work. For whatever reason, I find it important to prioritize them. Perhaps I am caught up in Matt's analysis paralysis.

First, while some could accept a small child in their lives at the age of 54, I could not. I know very well that it would only cause total frustration in my life. My daughter offered that the toddler would probably never live with her father, but I disagree. When she grows up a little, she may want to. Even though I know Mike would not want the responsibility, he would be only too willing to say yes and put that responsibility on me. That is the first, very important issue, and one that is so personally hurtful.

The next biggest issue for me is Mike's not being interested in providing the kind of help I want in keeping up a home. He has no interest and no ability. He never learned to fix anything, and he depends on me to fix things for him.

I am the one who checks out his car mechanically. I am the one to tell him that he needs new tires. I am the one to tell him that it's only tar on his car and he should just get some rubbing compound and rub it out.

Does he do this? No. No interest in the matter at all. This is not at all what I want in a man. I want a man who is capable of changing a tire on the roadside if need be, one who is willing and capable of hanging drapes, helping me move furniture, and keeping the outdoors respectable. This is not Mike. We're not even talking close. We are light years away from a congenial partnership of adulation and respect. This is the second, really big issue with me. Feel the anger?

In retrospect, early in the relationship, I recall this conversation clearly. I had just had a load of field stone delivered. Part of the load contained rocks from 2 to 5 inches in diameter, and some were 6 to 10 inches for decoration. I had moved several tons of these stones myself a couple of years prior, and it was time, I felt, to complete the landscaping. Mike had ever so kindly said that he would help me.

When the stones arrived, he planted himself firmly on the couch to watch a baseball game. I moved the stones.

I knew that he was tired and saw that he quickly drifted off to sleep. I was slightly irritated, but would not expect anyone to work when they were tired.

A second day brought an outright renege of his offer. He didn't feel like it. I politely packed up some lunch meat that he had bought and said he should take it with him and watch the game at his apartment.

This got a turnaround response. He now was willing to share in the work, but not until I had gone into that undertone rage. My words to him were emphatic and precise, "This is what will break us."

I let him know that I was not willing to allow him to lay around and enjoy the pleasant surroundings while I worked to make them more beautiful. He managed to get back in my good graces, but the remainder of the pile of field stone remains. Not once did he say, "We have nothing else going today, so why don't we get the rest of that landscaping done for you?"

Really, am I dreaming or what?

Thirdly, should I tolerate a weakness of an addiction? No matter how sweet and honest this man is, he is trouble and he is work. I adore him, his sincerity and his thoughtfulness, but gambling is intolerable.

And the newest incident of contention is that weed he smoked, given to him by a friend. That is another point of real concern. He ever so delicately offered it to me to share on our last weekend away, but was not pushy.

When I inquired about it recently, I learned that he had occasionally smoked it over a two-week period until it was gone. His honesty is the only thing to be admired.

My frustration is mounting. This man has no ambition, no desire to excel, and is coasting through life. Granted, this is what he needs at this point in time, but I dare say it will never be any different. This has been a fun ride. A wild excursion!

Now I must find a way to address these matters without causing him pain.

Chapter Twenty-Seven

The Melding of the Souls

As time has passed, the shared souls seemed to have settled more into their own beings. I have no way of knowing what is going on in Matt's life, but Mike's is not showing so many of Matt's personality traits.

The frequent calls have tapered off to one or less per day, so they are certainly under more control than Matt's ever were. As I review the traits of these two men, I am still comparing their likeness. What I am finding is the number of character traits that have returned to their distinctive owners. Mike is now having his own individuality.

There haven't been any more events of buy and sell of ridiculous items, only the purchase of an exorbitantly expensive room with a Jacuzzi for the night and two over-priced football tickets for a sell-out game. The room was a simple matter of supply and demand, and the tickets were not priced much over the original cost. I didn't feel that either were out-of-control issues.

I could see that both men lacked real ambition to get ahead in careers. They both seemed to hold back due to fear of failure. When they excelled, it was because of their innate ability, not their concerted effort.

Matt, however, was always quite motivated about his personal endeavors and was extremely creative and inventive. Follow-through was sometimes a problem, due to lack of development money, but the ideas were endless.

Mike may have exhibited more drive in his younger years, but today he is quite content to ring doorbells for sales as he walks from door to door. The idea that they might promote him into a better job does not appear to agree with his current nonchalant habits. The thought of a job demanding more of his free time is not at all appealing.

Matt was certainly more of a homemaker, as taking care of his own home was part of his life. Mike couldn't be bothered, and doesn't want the responsibility. He wants a simple life, and wouldn't have the financial means anyway. Matt liked a simple life as well, but had adapted to a regimented career in the corporate world, a family and home.

While Mike told me that he loved to dress up, I find that he now would much rather dress casually. He is only too content to wear white socks when he should wear dark, and dark shoes with shorts when he should wear white. He does, however, dress up regularly when we go out for the evening.

Matt, on the other hand, was always impeccably dressed, wore a suit well, and was finely pressed. He even wore dress shirts with jeans and always looked marvelous. He was one of those men that could do a dirty job dressed up and end up clean.

Both men are extremists at picking seating in a restaurant. It was not uncommon for Matt to move us three to four times before he found the best seat in the house. He was careful to select a place where we would be comfortable and have privacy. Mike does the same thing, but for different reasons. Mike wants to see the TV screen perfectly in each establishment and have enough space for himself as to not be irritated; the romantic mode for us is not even a factor.

Both of these men like their women to look good on their arms. Matt appreciated nice clothing, but was truly in favor of the visual stimulus of women's attire. Silk stockings, nice lingerie, and garter belts were what he liked to see. I was not that type of woman, but tried to please him. I loved the nice lingerie, but found stockings with garter belts terribly uncomfortable. He even bought me a jar of sparkles to wear for special occasions.

I have worn the sparkles to go out with Mike three times, but he never notices. I'd say they probably weren't that obvious, but my daughter came in the door one evening, just prior to our leaving the house, and said, "Oh, sparkles. How nice!"

Now that the two so-identical personalities have found their own persuasion, I am left to wonder what that was all about. True, they have their similarities, but my feeling is that the point was made, it served its purpose, and—what was it?

As stated by Gwenn, perhaps we were brought together *to have fun*. We did that. My feeling was that there was some karmic work to complete, and that it had something to do with the acceptance and responsibility of children.

Matt had abandoned his responsibility to his children too long because of the time he spent with me, and when his debts were called in, we parted. Mike, on the other hand, appears to have good relationships with two of his girls, but the third is seemingly irreparable. They don't have any communication at all, and I believe she, the eldest daughter, has disowned Mike. I have tried to suggest how he might make contact, but thus far that has been ignored.

My current thinking, since the relationship appears to be approaching an end mark, is that I am to learn something from this scenario. Matt left me to be a better father to his children. He did not want my assistance or interference in handling this responsibility. I am certain that he loved me very much when we parted, leaving me wanting.

Now, here I am with a man of similar family background. We have so many good things together, but he doesn't meet my expectations. His lifestyle doesn't meet my personal goals, and his likeness for absolute freedom from responsibility does not settle well with me.

Even though I was crazy in love to start, I have taken several giant steps back as each learned development of

Mike's life has taken its toll on the relationship. Am I now, somehow, to know what it feels like to love someone and not want the encompassing situation for my life? Was this what Matt really backed away from?

Or was the real lesson to make Mike handle his own responsibility of his young child, and not depend on his mate as he always did in the past? Is that why I was given those adamant feelings of rejection toward her? Was I supposed to feel that way in order to help his karma?

It appears that Mike is tackling each of his other hardships by himself, the bankruptcy and the back taxes. Perhaps responsibility is the lesson he is to learn.

Chapter Twenty-Eight

The Changing Sphere

My secondary vision always had a watchful eye. It saw Mike's sphere leave its upright position and take a tumble. It appeared to have broken loose from its axis and was rolling around. It wasn't thrashing around, so I knew that he wasn't in that much trouble. He was somewhat out of control, I could see, but was still seated at the bottom. The top had broken loose, which is what kept it upright. I could tell that his mental state was in turmoil. On the surface, I would never know; he appeared to be fine. I wouldn't have any idea of the disorientation that was going on inside of him if it weren't for this inner vision that I could see.

I talked to him about it. He agreed; that is just how he felt. He was also amazed that I could be that physic to see that image and know that something was going on with him. I explained that I could see visions such as this all of the time, but not necessarily on demand. Sometimes I would even see motion pictures going on in my head during meditation.

He had been in this state since he received the letter from the Internal Revenue Service. The tax accountant had told him to call the IRS and report that he wanted to take care of his debt, and the interaction had upset him terribly. He told me that he would much rather pay the money for the tax accountant to handle the entire matter and relieve him of the anxiety. We both agreed that peace of mind was a priceless commodity.

I not only saw Mike's symbolic object in a changed state, there were two others that had recently come into view. Gwenn, whose manifestation has changed many times, sometimes comes to me as an action, without a clear representation of her. I just know that it is Gwenn. This time I see her doing somersaults, and then springing back upright, somersaults, and then upright. I knew that whatever hoops she was jumping through, no doubt at work, she was resilient enough to get through it all right. When I talked to her, she, too, confirmed my analysis. Work had presented some very political hoops, and she had managed to get through them and still come out standing.

The third image that passed through my mind was of my friend, Jon. He is a gentleman who preferred going home to his Absolute vodka over my company, and with whom I have remained friends. He now lives in Texas, where he had previously bought a home and still owned it. He had left it occupied by a girlfriend who would take care of it while he was assigned work here in Michigan. Now that he has been forced to retire, he has moved there permanently and the girlfriend has moved out.

I thought that I would never hear from him again, but he made the effort to call me several months ago. I knew that he would be admitting himself into a dry-out facility upon his return to Texas, as he had shared his plan with me. I thought of him during the time that this was going on, and saw in my mind's eye that he was going through detox. I also knew when his misery was over.

As thoughts of him passed through my mind, I saw him standing alone, as I had seen him before, but as a taller boy than the last time. The bad news was that he was still holding onto a security blanket. I worried that he was unable to let go of the drinking and may have slipped back into his old habits.

We never discussed his treatment when he called me, as I felt it was in poor taste to bring it up. I didn't want to have it always be the focal point of our conversation. I'm sure he would like to forget it himself.

From Another Planet

Chapter Twenty-Nine

From Another Planet

Just when I was beginning to think that Mike wasn't bi-polar, and that he wasn't showing any real signs of losing control or eccentricity, as many manics do, I was again reminded of what deeply seated problems this disorder presented. And, I was just beginning to get comfortable that Matt's soul sharing space in Mike's body had ended, and that Mike was now his own person.

Even the tests that Gwenn had suggested I perform hadn't worked. She had wanted me to try to reach Mike telepathically to see if we were connected, and after I had succeeded, to then try to reach Matt to see if he was still *home*, or as if to say, could I still reach him in his own body. I never could reach Mike, so I was not able to complete the exercise.

When I told that to Gwenn she said, "Then your soul and Mike's soul may not be connected."

"That may be true," I said. "But I really think I have such a block on being close to Mike that I can't do it."

"Oh, a block—well that would certainly be in the way. That may be why," she said. "I still feel he is not of this earth somehow. I've always said that. Why don't you try something more simple. Instead of trying to get any kind of spiritual dialog, just try telling him telepathically to do something that is not too out of the ordinary, just something he should do in a short time frame."

So, I tried. Mike and I had been talking about his having some moles on his face removed because they kept becoming irritated, and he seemed to be moving forward on a lot of things that he needed to do. I concentrated on his seeing a physician and taking care of them the following week. He did not. He took care of some other pressing matter that was important, but not the moles. I failed to make contact again.

I may not be able to connect that way, but there is certainly some connectivity. There are times that I feel that I absolutely must talk to him. I must hear his voice to feel whole. He doesn't have to talk about anything in particular, but I must talk to him, and I do. He is almost always reachable by cell phone, and I make the connection. After I hear his voice, I feel right again.

Some of the same things that are preventing me from getting too close to Mike are also heavy on his mind. I have learned that it is not only the personal bankruptcy and the back taxes owed to the Federal Government that are issues, but the fact that he had been claiming ten exemptions for the past two years when he only had two. This would now catch up with him and he would owe more money.

How can you feel close to someone so irresponsible unless you are willing to just take care of them? The pressure of knowing there would be less money available to him for our entertainment was what was bothering him. Entertainment was his life's ambition.

"You know I won't have as much money to spend on us pretty soon, don't you?" he asked.

"Yes," I answered. "But you could work more."

"Oh, yes, I guess I could do that. That would help."

As it was, he was probably only working 20 to 25 hours a week for 25 sales, which brought him a comfortable income. True, he made 25 sales to the other salesmen's 18 - 20 sales in 40 hours, but he knew how to work smarter. He was actually capable of making twice the income in half the time.

He quickly forgot what I had just said and continued speaking. He was still perplexed as to how to make this money shortage work. He carried on his conversation saying, "You know if I had the money, I would wine you and dine you all of the time, but I'm just not going to have that money anymore. How would you feel about sharing expenses?"

Well, I never! I could not believe what I was hearing with my own ears! This was not a man at all. What did he think of me? Did he think we were married? I didn't know if I was more furious, hurt, or just outraged. I clearly let him know that was not acceptable. We never actually wined and dined anyway, as our outings were always on a more moderate budget. I told him that he could just stay home, or we could plan some activities together at home that would not cost money, but I was not willing to let him spend his money freely all week long, and have me pay for the weekend.

How can someone grow up in this world and not learn what it means to be a man?

He curiously accepted this retaliated comment and calmly continued. "Do you feel the same way about us spending vacations together?" He certainly stayed focused! I think that is one thing manics usually cannot do.

I explained that I wouldn't expect him to have to cover the entire vacation for us unless he wonderfully won a trip for two someplace. In actuality, I preferred when a man prepares to provide for the whole trip and is then pleasantly surprised when the lady covers some major expenses. Disappointed in him, I agreed that if the trip were not too expensive that I would be glad to help out.

Two days later, Mike continued calling as if nothing major had transpired. I was still steaming, still hurt, and disappointed in him. I tried letting him know, but I could tell that he just wasn't getting it. I told him that I was still very upset about our conversation, but that I thought I had figured out part of the problem. I would discuss it when we got together.

In my mind, I rationalized the essence of his personality. He had spent his entire lifetime trying not to be responsible for himself, and this was just one more experience that he did not want to face alone. He wanted me to take responsibility for his shortcomings and help him out! I would only be enabling him if I were to do so.

By the next evening, he had had time to internalize the last few days' conversations, and was extremely interested in meeting with me to give me a big apology. He had obviously just figured out what he had done.

We did not connect by phone that evening; however, he called me the next day to exclaim, "Did you know that men are from Mars and women are from Venus?"

"Yes, I had heard that," I responded. We agreed to meet that evening for dinner so that we could talk. I thought I must confirm to Gwenn that he was, indeed, from another planet.

When we met, I made him go through his apology and reasoning before I countered with any of my thoughts. He explained that he had a big problem with logic, he knew, and that even in business he had made several real blunders because of missing common sense issues.

Then it hit me. This was a manic's problem. A faux pas would be a natural thing. "Do you remember when we met and I told you that you were manic-depressive?"

"Yes," he said.

"And I told you that there would probably be some disconnect in logic, but that I hadn't placed what it was yet?

"Yes," he said again.

"Well, that's it. It's that common sense thing. That's the missing link that I talked about." It was as if Mike had just been born and had no experience from which to draw upon. "That's the disconnect," I concluded. Then I explained what I knew about this shortcoming.

I recalled how Matt's logic disconnect was in what is termed analysis paralysis. In regard to me, I could never be absolutely right for him, even though he knew better, because he was never done analyzing. There was a disconnect between the problem and its solution. It use to anger me that he could logically figure all of this out and explain it to me, but he couldn't solve it for us. I couldn't understand what his problem was if he understood it and could explain it to me.

Now I could explain it to Mike. I told him that he could not blame himself for this disconnect. He was born with it. It was not a behavior that he could learn or correct. It was, as explained to me, an actual gap of reasoning in the brain. It was a misfire; it couldn't make the connection.

It happened again a few days later on another matter, and again he stayed intently focused on his reasoning to the exclusion of how I might feel about the matter. This time we both recognized it within a day and worked it out. He thanked me for understanding him.

Later in conversation that day, he was talking about visiting a company and falling in love with a picture they had on a wall. He inquired about purchasing it and found that it was not for sale. He persisted, and was able to buy the picture.

"Thank you, God, for reaffirming that I am still, for whatever reason, dealing with Matt's soul in Mike's body." Matt had done the same thing with a picture in a restaurant one morning when we were having breakfast! That was a pretty clear sign, don't you think? You would have to agree, not too many people do this sort of thing.

Chapter Thirty

Why it all Happened

As is becoming the standard for God's sending me messages, and he knows very well that I'm slow to catch on, I now feel that all of the many negative aspects of my relationship with Mike were planned. I wasn't supposed to stay in love with him. God made sure that I wouldn't try to just accept one or two things that weren't exactly right and compensate, or make allowances for the shortcomings. No, He would be sure that there were too many to excuse, too many to overlook.

Mike has stated more than once that he has learned a lot from this relationship. I probably can't expound on what all of those things are, but among them are the principles of taking care of a lady. Truly, despite his shortcomings in this area, he is positively the most endearing man and works harder on a relationship than most men would. He has had three wives to practice on before meeting my acquaintance, and has had much self-improvement training through lectures and spiritual church talks by his own seeking. Surely that has paid off in some respects.

Additionally, since his total assets are actually liabilities, I have at least instilled in him the need to save money, and the fact that he only has ten years to save for retirement. He is taking my commentary to heart and is already on the right path. However, I don't really think he understands, and the purpose of life insurance surely escapes him.

My original suspicions of the reason for his partnering with me was to work out his ill relationships with one or more of his children. This has not proven to be true. He appears to have a great relationship with the two younger daughters. The eldest daughter, who doesn't speak to him, does not appear to be a forerunner in his list of near-term needed achievements. He has so many that are needed, in terms of survival, that I can almost understand why this is true.

The timing for this last daughter relationship to be resolved may very well happen in the early fall of this year. His middle daughter is engaged to be married then, and the oldest daughter and Mike will no doubt be in attendance. It is my hope that both will be more receptive to some interchange of conversation or breaking down of the walls which have been so sturdily built. I hope that this is true, for Mike should have most of his other bad karma worked out. I cannot speak for the gambling addiction, however, as he claims that this still exists.

My lesson to be learned from this relationship might be more profound. In my relationship with Matt, it was he who pulled away because of having family debts that had come due. His primary concern was to parent his youngest son. He found it imperative not to include me in his life in order to do this, for reasons I am not to understand. With Mike, I have found the tables to be turned. It is he with a young daughter, and I am not willing to take on that family debt in my life. Perhaps that will be a family debt that he will someday need to address.

In my analysis, the Matt and Mike interchangeability indications are undeniable. There is enough evidence that the transfer of the soul did take place, and I was to learn how it felt in reverse in order to understand Matt's actions. I do not fully understand, but feel that I must accept.

If I were to put it in words of something that he just couldn't do, whether he understood his reasons or not, just as my position with Mike and his little girl is something I felt I just couldn't do, then perhaps I am on the right track. The circumstances were presented probably as closely as they could be. Surely, I can rationalize that Matt's responsibility to his son should remain his without my intervention, and Mike's responsibility to his daughter should be his alone as well.

How else could an irresponsible personality prove himself worthy? I think I always knew this, but I have just come to the realization of what each of their missions may be in this life. I think they are both here to learn to take this responsibility.

Chapter Thirty-One

Ellen Has a Ball!

I went to a Christmas dinner at my friend, Gwenn's, house, and we made an exchange of gifts. One of my gifts included two books that she had purchased from a used bookstore. The paperback was on developing your physic power, and a larger, hardcover book was about visions and prophecies. The word *visions* was of immediate interest, as I was trying to learn more about the experiences that I had. I began reading it that evening after returning home.

Somewhat disappointed in my early findings, although it stated that many of the incidents predicted had come true, it did not explain how the prophets saw those visions or how they came about their prophecies. It wasn't until a much later chapter in the book, which contained other mediums' work, that I found what it was that I had been looking for.

Of particular interest was a chapter that contained various means of scrying, and it explained that scrying was looking into anything that reflected back. This could be a pool of water, a mirror, or a crystal ball. The person who described using the ball specified what she saw in a vision that exactly mirrored what I see. What she said was that sometimes she saw a single static image, sometimes the vision would fade out and another would appear in a series like a slide show, and sometimes it was like watching a motion picture! I was ecstatic. I hadn't read anything where anyone had described visions the way that I saw them, and I had not even used a crystal ball.

She also went on to say that when you peer into a crystal ball, the ball itself disappears and then the psychic vision is forthcoming. I had to have one now. I wanted one badly. I saw visions in my mind's eye without the ball, so getting the ball, I felt, would only enhance what I could see. The book stated:

> Within five minutes, the ball becomes opaque and milky, like clouds passing. When the clouds disperse, images may form. They might appear as a single static image, in a series like a slide show, or as a full-blown movie-like presentation.
>
> When the vision appears, the ball disappears . . . it is difficult to say 'seen in the crystal.'

Within the next day or so I had an appointment to have my hair cut in town, and I knew that there was a psychic store a couple of blocks from the hair salon. I arrived on time for my hair appointment, which was at 6:00 p.m. Almost everything in town closes up by five or six o'clock, so upon finishing having my hair cut, I decided to ride by the physic store to check their hours. I wanted to know if I could make it there before they closed if I came directly after work.

When I was parking the car, I could see the open sign in the psychic store window. It looked fairly dark in there, so I couldn't be sure. They were still open!

I went inside. The young man said, "We're closing, so unless you know what you want, you should probably come back another time."

"I know what I want," I said. "I want a crystal ball."

"Do you want glass or crystal?" he asked.

"Glass, I said," knowing that I had just read that either works and glass is cheaper.

"Glass is certainly more affordable and works just the same," he stated. "Are you going to use it, or is it just for decoration?"

"Oh, I'm going to use it," I said.

He then brought out both types so that I could see them. The glass ball was clear, like I had always seen in movies. The crystal one had white, milky lines running through the entire ball—not what I pictured at all.

"The glass is fine," I said. "How much is it?"

The price was $69.00. Still not cheap, but SOLD! The ball made of crystal was nearly $400.00. Satisfied, I made my purchase.

The salesman appeared to run the store with his father, who was seated on a stool behind the counter. The father explained that I should wash the ball in warm salt water. That would clean off all of the other spirits that might be there from others handling the ball.

He continued to tell me that it worked best when placed on a dark cloth, like velvet.

"Okay," I said.

"Do you want any other tips," he asked?

"Of course," I answered. "I know very little about using the ball. I just know that I want one."

"Use the ball in a dimly lit room," he said. Place a lit candle behind you, but don't let the candle's light reflect in the ball. That would only distract you. The candle behind you will make the ball appear dark. After you look into the ball, the ball itself will disappear. Then you will see the visions."

"Really," I said. "That is exactly what I just read."

"I'm telling you that because the first time it happened to me, it really scared me. It might take you a few times using it before you see anything, though."

"Oh. Thank you. I get visions without the ball, so I'm anxious to use it."

"I see," he said. "Then you will probably get a vision the first or second time you use it."

"Have you any other tips?" I asked.

"Yes. Don't let anyone else touch the ball. Keep it just for you. They can look at it, but don't let them touch it. I suggest you keep it out of the way where others won't be tempted."

With that, I took my precious and heavy package out of the store, placed it carefully in my car, and went home.

I had no intention of using the ball right away. I would wait until the mood and circumstances felt right before trying. Excited about my purchase, I quickly told Mike and Gwenn of my expenditure over the telephone, also explaining that I had no plans for its immediate use.

I asked Gwenn if she had any leftover fabric from the plush, dark-blue velvet quilt she had just made me for my birthday, but she did not.

"That's okay," I said. "I can buy some dark velvet. I just thought it would be the perfect thing if you had some left over."

"You can place the ball on the blanket on your lap," she offered. "That should work for you."

The suggestion was all that I needed. Later that evening, in my somewhat sleepy state, I took my freshly washed ball from its resting place and put it in my lap on the dark, blue velvet blanket.

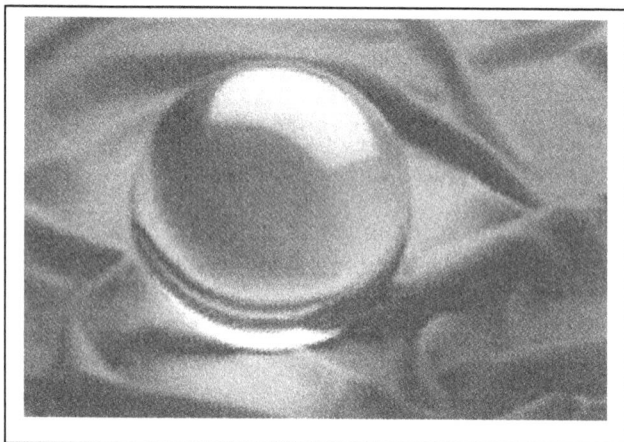

Crystal Ball

I had already lit a candle, as I often do in the evening, and now placed it carefully behind me. The room was very dark, but I really didn't expect to see anything in the ball anyway.

I stared into the ball. I concentrated on Mike's and my relationship, the weight of its existence resting heavily upon me. I asked what was to become of the relationship, how long would it last, and how would it end. I realized that was a lot to ask, and furthermore, I had no idea if one should ask a question at all!

Within seconds, the ball disappeared. A pelican appeared. I recognized it by its beak. Then it was gone.

Pelican

I saw ocean water and waves. I also saw a vivid blue sky with white fluffy clouds.

Mike and I had tentatively arranged to take a trip to South Beach, Florida, but it had been placed on hold due to a pending job opportunity for advancement thought to include training the same week that we had planned to go.

I vaguely remember other scenes of Florida come and go in the ball, but I can't tell you what I saw. Entranced in what I was seeing, I thought I should begin to question what was being presented. Then I saw a glass elephant. "Now where did that come from?" I thought. "What did that mean?" I wondered. Then it faded out.

Glass Elephant

Now I could see nothing. I stretched my eyes open as wide as I could, to assure myself that they were indeed open. Disbelieving, I tried again. I was still wide-eyed, and could see nothing at all! No crystal ball. Just a blank screen!

I waited. I stared into nothingness. The world looked totally black.

My hands reached until I felt the crystal ball. I picked it up and placed it back on the glass tray where I had put it after its cleaning, blew out the candle and went to bed.

The next day I rationalized that the trip to Florida was going to happen. Something was going to change in regard to our trip being placed on hold for the job training.

Sure enough, the company had erred. The interview and training would take place the following month. Mike was told to take his vacation with his lady friend and to enjoy himself.

I now wonder about the blank screen. Does the relationship have nothing to offer after the trip? I have not inquired into the ball again. Perhaps after the trip I will have more time.

Chapter Thirty-Two

The Gods are Near Again

Throughout the relationship with Mike, I have never really lost touch with the spirits of others I have cared about. I somehow always knew, among the mayhem of an ultra-exciting relationship with Mike, that it was never intended to last.

There are times when I am plagued by messages from reading license plates, of all things, that tell me what Matt is doing in his life and with whom. For instance, they have indicated that Matt's current girlfriend's name is Fran. He often compares her to me. She and I have similar qualities. We would both make good mates for him. He will be in Florida sometime within January or February of this year as well as myself. We will not meet up.

These are things that could be proven or disproven, but I do not want to initiate the contact to find out. The year before last provided yet another story. My license plate information told me that Matt had a van, or had access to a van, and was going to New York for New Year's Eve. He had a disagreement with Fran, and they almost didn't go, but then worked it out.

I also have a watchful eye on Steve's symbolic representation as well, which is not at all attractive at this time. He would be embarrassed to learn that the messages that I have been receiving are associated with the porcelain throne.

Most of the time I see him sitting on the throne, and there is a blockage. He has been unable to get past that for quite some time now. I'm not certain what he needs to get past yet, but more than likely it is the loss of his marriage or the ensuing loss of his ill mother.

In any event, this type of vision should not be connected with an educated, highly accomplished, and good-looking man as Steve.

For months I could tell that the Gods were near me, and by that I mean God and his angels. Although they were always close by, on two distinct occasions I could actually feel their presence. Each time I would be hopeful that they would decide that Steve and I might reunite, but they always left undecided.

Then one day I realized that I could feel the Gods getting further away, fleeting. Fleeting away from me. I did not like the feeling as it represented the loss of Steve. I cared so much because Steve was a soul mate, and we have traveled through life together in one or more other lifetimes. Two and a half years after only six months of dating, and I have clearly not eradicated him from my heart.

I very seldom remember dreaming, but I had a dream of Steve and Lillian. Steve had introduced me to Lillian, so she was the connection between us now. Sketchy as dreams are, I remember having made a chicken dish and taking it to Lillian's house for dinner. There were leftovers, which she kept. I had also written a letter to her on colorful parchment paper, which would be strange as she was legally blind. The letter contained some words about the dinner as well as some feelings about Steve and his disappearance from my life. In the dream, Steve was at her home a day or two later and finished the meal with her. He had somehow found the letter I had written, and had responded back to me on the same piece of paper, between my lines.

He wrote that the dinner had been delicious. He also apologized for the events that caused him to leave my life. He tried to explain, in proper terms, what his feelings were at that time. When I awakened, I tried to find the words that he used in the dream. The word I was stuck on was either "charlatan," meaning "fraud," or "chivalry," explained as "virtues of honesty and morality."

This truly explained the reason why he backed away when he did. He was going through a divorce when I met him and had been separated from his wife. At the time he stopped seeing me, the divorce was nearly over, but his virtues and morality would not allow the relationship to develop while he was still legally married. That would have been deceitful in his eyes.

He had suggested that we would get together again in the fall, but I didn't hear from him. By fall, someone had introduced him to another lady and he later married her.

Chapter Thirty-Three

Stolen Goods

It was New Year's Eve, and Mike and I had plans for a moderate evening of entertainment. He explained that it was his fault that he had not put money aside for a more extravagant evening, but that we would still go out and have a great time.

I understood his personality enough to know that he was sincere, and as long as we could go out, I would be happy. His original plan would have been to make reservations at an average-priced establishment that had live music. We would then retire at a nearby hotel for the night so that we didn't have to drive home so late, have a leisurely breakfast in the morning, and then return home. Now, with limited funds, Mike was planning an evening at a place that had a D.J., dancing, and then we would come directly back to my place. That was perfectly fine with me.

I passed on the information to both my son, Doug, and his fiancée, Janelle, of what we were doing for the evening. I tried to encourage them to go out, as they seldom did. On the day before New Year's Eve, I received a call from my son to ask if they and another couple could join us. The other couple was Doug's salesman and his long-term, live-in girlfriend, Loraine, who was also Janelle's mother. I liked them both, so I was excited about the evening. I also knew that Mike would not mind the intervention of additional company.

We were off to a great evening. Because of Mike's tight funds, he alerted me to the fact that our dinner had been pre-paid, and that he would only be carrying fifty dollars with him for our drinks and valet. While I knew this would be more than enough, I was responsible for the invitation of four other people, and I didn't want him to become financially embarrassed should our drinks be placed on a much larger bill with our company. I therefore put another fifty dollars in my wallet.

The evening's entertainment turned out to be a disaster. The music banged on and on, with no rhythm, and would only appeal to a much younger age group. George remarked that we were well represented with a broad age spread. Janelle was in her twenties, Doug his thirties, Loraine in her forties, and Mike and I in our fifties. George was in his early sixties. Janelle was probably the only one who could relate to the music.

Disappointed in the music, Mike called a nearby restaurant and succeeded in getting us reserved space at the bar for the rest of the evening. We ate our dinner, which was actually an okay buffet, and exited for the next place. When we arrived, we were able to sit at a couple of small cocktail tables, which were near the dance floor. The music was live, which pleased Mike, and much more to all of our liking. It was a definite save for the evening.

I not only had more money in my wallet than I would normally carry on such a night, I also stupidly took my brand new camera that Doug and Janelle had given me for Christmas. I wanted to show my appreciation of the gift, feeling that with six people at the table, all would be safe. Wrong.

All was fine until after the New Year. Mike and I were dancing when our company of four decided to leave to go home. My son approached me on the dance floor and kindly explained that he was moving my purse and camera to their table, against a wall, so that it would be less accessible to someone's greedy hands. I thanked him and said goodnight to them all.

Matt and I finished the dance, and went directly to the table, which now had been completely cleared. There were no empty glasses, no ashtrays, as all of our company smoked, no purse, no camera, and no prescription glasses that Mike had left on the table.

We approached the management for their assistance, but to no avail. Everything was gone. Mike and I had to go to Doug's house that evening and wait for him to return home in order to get a key to my house. He had driven George and Loraine home, and my keys were, of course, in the stolen purse.

I felt violated. The culprit not only had my purse with house and car keys , he or she had my address. Janelle provided me with a steel baseball bat to keep at my bedside until I could have the locks changed on my house.

No further incident occurred, but the locks were changed, and my driver's license, bank cards and credit cards were replaced. Mike and I made a police report on New Year's Day, and revisited the restaurant where the event took place. Our hope was that one of the wait staff had cleared the table thinking that we had left, and had put all of our things safely away. The management was perturbed that we were bothering them, and I knew then that we would not get any assistance.

The strange thing that happened from this revisit was a wave of psychic images that crossed my mind. I could see the purse and camera together in my mind's eye , but not the missing eyeglasses. I could see that the purse and camera had been placed under an object that was flat and rounded at the end or edge.

I pictured rocks, outside, that were smooth and flat, but that did not feel right. In my vision I also saw a small oblong opening, through which these items had been inserted, side-by-side. I didn't know what that opening was, but saw such a slot on the dumpster behind the restaurant where Mike and I parked. We tried to see if there were any discarded items in there, but the dumpster was too high, and we would not see into it. It also would have been difficult for someone to throw items over the top easily.

"Wouldn't it be wonderful to be able to solve this yourself?" exclaimed Gwenn!

"Yes, but a slim chance that would be," I countered.

I could later picture this person's house. It was an older brick home. There were hundreds of similar brick homes in the area of the restaurant with no way to trace this one. Of course, the vision was too scant to picture it exactly.

I felt that the home was located on a street that began with the letter L, or at least had an L prominent in the sound, as in Elmwood. So what. I didn't even know what city.

Still later, I could see this person's car. It was an old, beat up, cream-colored Chrysler with squared fenders. Again, nothing much to go on.

While still in the parking lot, I played Sherlock writing down the license number of a peculiar person lurking around the back of the restaurant's dumpster when Mike and I arrived. He subsequently went into the back door of the kitchen, but when I questioned the manager of the business about him, he deliberately made me wait twenty minutes and then denied his ever having been there. I could appreciate his loyalty to his help, but I was getting nowhere.

I've now laid the issue to rest and will replace the camera shortly.

Chapter Thirty-Four

Weeble-Wobble

As customary with my normal activities, I am given the internal image of what a person's current state is in life when it is important to do so. I saw Mike's sphere, the symbolic representation of his world, in a rocking, rolling state. It resembled the toy of an egg-shaped character some years back, with the advertisement which said, "Weebles wobble but they don't fall down."

I relayed this information to Mike.

"Is that bad?" he asked.

"No, not necessarily," I replied. "You have been shaken by the recent job disappointment, but you're still on your feet," I explained.

Mike and two co-workers had been selected as the top producers, and were eligible for interview outside of their current division. He was elated. Scared, but elated. The fear was due to his many failures in the past, whether or not he was fully responsible for them.

He immediately sought out a new therapist, feeling that he could not manage his life in a new endeavor without one. He needed the guidance and someone to talk to.

They Weeble and they Wobble
but they Don't Fall Down

He was able to find one near his home, and one with
whom he had immediate rapport. This was good. It was
also appropriate that he accidentally found one who
happened to specialize in bi-polar disorders, the manic-
depressive personality to which I have many times

referred. He is comfortable with this therapist and has now undergone countless sessions and hours of testing to determine his needs.

There was a mix-up in communication with the jobs that were to be singled out for these three fellows, and two of the three had been told that no openings existed at the present time. The third person did manage to obtain a position at his own seeking, outside the normal channels.

Mike was shaken at this, tried to seek out a position on his own within the company, and was severely reprimanded by his leader. Then the second man found a new job and was placed, leaving Mike alone, the top performer, and the only one who had not been placed.

With that information and a heavy heart, he weeble-wobbled out of state on a vacation with me to Florida. The missed job, and his failing to obtain one on his own, burdened him heavily. While on vacation, he tried to make the right contacts back at his work place, but had not been given good information and was unable to reach the right people.

I explained that there was some reason why he was not able to do that. He should not worry, as the timing was probably not right. I told him that he would most likely end up in a better position for having missed the current opportunity, and the other two fellows would be envious. He seemed somewhat satisfied by my assessment.

On Christmas Eve, I met Mike at his church for a candlelight service. It was a lovely thing to do on Christmas Eve. His spirits were somewhat unstable, but the service was comforting to him.

Since this was a progressive, non-denominational church, part of this service contained music that I personally felt was out of place. I quipped about having gone to a rock concert. The church appeared to try to reach everyone with their individual interests, and I watched as some members of the group stood and rocked back and forth to the music.

If I had not been present, Mike would have joined those who were rocking and rolling. He loved that kind of music and enjoyed it being part of the service. Others sat quietly through this portion of the program.

We spoke about it later, and he admitted that if I hadn't been there, he would have been one of the standers in the group. I said, "They may as well have said, 'Will all of the manics please stand up.'"

With that he laughed. "Oh," he said, "I guess I should have realized that's where my interest in music comes from."

"Not necessarily," I said. "Lots of people enjoy music."

He continues to weeble and wobble, but he is standing more erect now and I'm sure will not fall down.

Chapter Thirty-Five

Second Enchantment

It was Monday evening, the evening before Mike and I were to leave for our trip to Florida. We had planned to stay at a hotel near the airport in order to make our early-morning departure easier. Excited to start the party early, he suggested that we meet at a restaurant on his side of town that was serving lobster at a special rate in their bar between 5:00 and 7:00 p.m.

We did, and it was great. While there, seated at the bar rail and overlooking the restaurant, I faced three gentlemen at a table below. The man directly facing me had a fair complexion, was handsome, and had shown a look of admiration toward me with a nod of approval. I quietly acknowledged him with a smile.

The evening continued with Mike and I engaged in light conversation, he bubbling over with concern of the ensuing job and of the trip. The gentleman and I continued to exchange glances, each with our own private fascination, as we sat in direct view of one another. The restaurant was nearly empty except for the bar area, as many had come to enjoy this lobster special.

When it was time to leave, Mike said that he would go get the check, since the waiter had not appeared for some time.

I said "Fine. I'll go to the ladies room and meet you back here."

I returned before Mike did, and the gentleman with whom I had been exchanging glances spoke to me.

"Where is your friend?" he inquired.

"He's getting the check," I said.

"Oh, I was hoping you could join us for a drink later."

"That would be wonderful," I said, "but I can't this evening."

"I understand," he said. "Maybe next time," which was perfectly timed with Mike's return.

Nothing was noticed. Nothing was said. The thought lingered for some time. I also reflected on the *smiling face* that had caught my glance while riding in the car with Mike that one evening. I knew this admiring man did not have the same charisma and charm of the smiling man, and he was not a soul mate. He was attractive and very appealing, however, and one I would not refuse to see again had I not had Mike in my life.

I privately assumed this was just a test of my stability and longevity in my relationship with Mike. Was it a sign of what was to come, an advance notice? Or was it just my luminescent appearance of happiness with Mike that made me more attractive?

Chapter Thirty-Six

The Meeting of Ellie

My son, Doug, was soon jilted in his relationship. He was devastated that his fiancée had become attracted to the limo driver hired for their wedding and was now seeing him. He found out by taping a phone conversation between them, permissible to do in your own home.

He was now trying to get out and get back into dating. He made friends with a fellow from work, and they chummed together going out and meeting the ladies. He soon met a young woman who had two children of her own from her first marriage. She had only been divorced a short time, but had a personality to win over anyone or any man. I liked her very well upon our first meeting.

Sunday was Labor Day, and Doug was bringing her over with her two children to have a barbecue. Mike and I had our usual Saturday night date, with him spending the night and spending Sunday morning with me.

Mike now had visitation with his daughter on Sunday, and since I was having children over anyway, for the first and only time in our relationship, I asked him if he would like to bring Ellie back for the day to play with the other girls.

I'm sure he could not resist the invitation, as it was one I had never extended before. The girls were all about the same age, and while this issue itself had always bothered me, I had resolved myself to the fact that it didn't have to matter, because Mike's relationship and mine were not ever going to be consummated. To extend the invitation now was perfectly harmless.

Mike accepted, and picked Ellie up at the usual time and brought her back to the house with permission from Ellie and Ellie's Mom.

When Mike returned with Ellie, I was busy in the kitchen baking peanut-butter cookies for the girls, as I felt they would enjoy them better than the dessert I was serving the adults. Children usually did better with cookies that they could pick up in their hands and take with them.

Ellie was an adorable child, with immeasurable beauty. She was darling, and I took to her immediately.

Mike said, "Ellie likes to bake, too. Can she help you?"

"Why certainly," I said. "Let me go get a stool for her to stand on so she can work here at the counter with me."

I returned with the stool, and Ellie climbed up so that she could help with the cookie making process. The mix was ready, and so I said, "Why don't you help me put them onto the cookie sheets, Ellie?" I then proceeded to show her how to fill the spoon.

She was happy to help and fill the spoon, and handed it to me to put on the cookie sheet. We worked out a team effort.

She was dressed in an adorable pinafore, something a treasured doll would wear. She looked like a delicate china doll, too, and was just as sweet as her father.

Soon after the cookies were done, Doug, the new girlfriend, Karen, and the other girls arrived. We all went outside to enjoy the yard and fresh air. I had previously gotten permission from my next door neighbor for the children to use their swing set.

"Sure," my neighbor had said. In fact, there is a small swimming pool you are welcome to fill and use, too. We are going to be gone all weekend, so you won't be bothering us at all."

I had asked Mike to fill the pool before going to pick up Ellie so that the water would at least be warm for the children. He did so, and when he came back into the house, I politely asked, "Did you recoil my neighbor's hose?"

He was irritated that I should ask, although I didn't feel that my question should have been taken with such offense.

"Of course. I know how to take care of a hose!" he angrily retorted. I had never experienced such a reaction from him before.

The rest of the day went fairly well, but other signs were there that Mike had little tolerance for my somewhat critical disposition. The relationship was over the "love and forgiveness stage" and into the "you are beginning to irritate me" time. I'm sure the reverse was also true, or I wouldn't have come across as harsh as I must have seemed.

The children were terribly slow to get acquainted. The two sisters were seemingly content to play with each other as they were accustomed, and a newcomer was totally unnecessary to their set. Ellie was extremely shy and watched the girls at a distance, not even trying to join in on their fun.

Mike and Ellie climbed up on the well-constructed wooden swing and slide set, and Mike assisted his daughter in using the slide. Ellie enjoyed it very much. I now was pushing the other two girls on the swings, with the little one more daring than all the rest to go higher and higher. I was clearly more afraid than she was. I would hate for anything to happen to any of them.

By evening, we were all inside in the living room, and the girls had finally made some form of acquaintance. Both sisters were extremely rough compared to Ellie, and I found myself protecting her from their pushing and grabbing. Ellie was afraid of their bold actions, and much more delicate than they were.

I adored Karen's two girls immensely. They had some endearing qualities of immediate closeness to me that

I've not experienced with any other children. I don't outwardly warm up to little ones, but upon first meeting her girls, they trustingly climbed up on my lap for my affection, immediately steeling my heart.

Now I had three little girls vying for my attention, each getting as close to me on the couch as they could. Karen's girls were on either side of me, and I could see Ellie's problem of losing out on my affection. When we sat down to dinner, she had already expressed to her father, "I want to sit with her," acknowledging that I had won her friendship.

Recognizing Ellie's dilemma, I reached for her hand and led her to the prime spot on my lap, now hopefully showing no partiality to any one of the three children. She was delighted, and comforted to know that she had not been left out.

At the end of the evening, I dared to remind Mike on two occasions to empty the swimming pool before leaving to take Ellie home. He ignored my requests.

Doug, when overhearing me, jumped up to take care of it. That was the kind of man I was use to having around me. Not one that had to be directed constantly.

I was outside in the yard the next day, and glanced at the hose on my next-door neighbor's house that Mike "certainly knew how to take care of," and began to roar with laughter.

Mike had replaced the hose all right. However, instead of coiling the hose around the hanger like everyone else I have ever known, he had replaced it by reversing it back and forth over the top of the hanger.

Chapter Thirty-Seven

A Message from Sabrina

As I go about my days, still enjoying the relationship with Mike, I am feeling just a little constrained by it. I know that my purpose with him is nearly fulfilled, and I wonder how I am going to approach breaking it off.

I don't feel Mike is going to face the need at all. He is seemingly comfortable in the relationship, and willing to let it go on as long as possible, even if not forever. I feel a break will be hurtful for both of us, but to let it go on for much longer will not be good. Each day I worry a little more about it. Each day I feel a little less comfortable with it, knowing that I should be moving on.

I not only rely on Gwenn for her support in such matters, as she and I serve as each other's conscience from time to time, but I rely on my favorite horoscope writer, Brady. Brady tells me not to be too content.

This week he writes:

> The person who is content with petty
> happiness will not attain great happiness.

Since he promised electrifying bliss with a little reach and stretch, I am more inclined to let my thoughts wander in that direction. I reflected upon the *smiling man* and *the admiring man*. I felt there was more out there for me.

Still, I worry about the hurt that will ultimately come from such a break, and just how to go about it.

One day on my way to work, clear thoughts of Sabrina crossed my mind. Sabrina was an acquaintance of the past, now deceased, who read my tarot cards during the period of my failing marriage.

Sabrina is also the one that Gwenn said would be the person to answer my question of what my purpose was in Mike's life. I was to ask her at some time when the circumstances were right, but I never did.

At the end of my reading with Sabrina, she offered:

> "You don't have to do anything;
> it will take care of itself."

And it did. A divorce followed, each step being driven by what I called an invisible hand. When the time was right, the right things happened. It was a driving force that put events into play, and things just happened.

On my drive to work this particular morning, along with a vision of her, Sabrina repeated these same words to me.

> "You don't have to do anything;
> it will take care of itself."

I then knew that the circumstances around Mike's and my relationship would just happen at the right time. I felt that time was drawing near.

I shared this feeling with Gwenn. I told her, "I think our karmic work together is nearly complete. I believe I was to see him through to stability, and he was to serve as a catalyst in delivering a message to me from Matt."

"I believe you are exactly right," proclaimed Gwenn. It was not often that she so openly agreed with me.

Since I had been negligent in actually asking Sabrina what my purpose was to be in Mike's life, even though I felt I knew, I now felt that I should ask her.

I could see her face. I could hear her voice, but I could not make out the words. I struggled. I strained to hear the words, but could not. Finally, a picture appeared in my mind.

The sphere was up on a stage, rocking to and fro. I was wearing a ballerina costume and toe shoes. I made my way up onto the platform, steadied the sphere, turned around, got down, and walked away. That was my answer. I was to steady the sphere, and then leave. I shall be on my way soon.

This weekend Mike said, in hopes of a new job soon, "Will you still love me when I become a business man?" He knew that his playful side would suddenly have to become more serious, and he would really have to work for a living.

"Yes, I will still love you," I replied.

"I guess you will. If you loved me just being a peddler, I suppose you will."

"I was supposed to be here to see you through," I said. "That's why I was put into your life." I wanted to say, our karmic work is almost done, but I didn't. I knew he would not understand, and I didn't feel that I wanted to explain what part he had played in mine.

Chapter Thirty-Eight

The New Job

Many months have passed since having the feeling that our karmic work together was drawing to a close. The "not having to do anything about it" was holding true. Ever so slowly, we were drifting apart. As relationships do, little things that one is so tolerant of when the excitement and happiness prevails were becoming slightly irritating and bothersome.

The new job came for Mike, but did not come easily. It was a fight to get it, which in itself was to deliver several messages, I am sure.

The pay method on the new job was once a month, and difficult to budget. Getting money in weekly, as he had in the past, was much easier to manage. Most could handle getting through the first three weeks with a tapering down of funds, but not Mike. After week one, he was dry.

My ultimate patience was ready, and I invited him over for steaks on the grill. Our plan was to go to By-the-Bay for soft drinks that evening. It wasn't that Mike was being frivolous with what he had; there just wasn't enough coming in. It was all he could do to pay his rent, child support, car payment, and car insurance. I knew this would be the way it would be for some time. The commission money that he used to get would not be there for quite a while.

The latter part of the evening was spent at By-the-Bay, dancing to live music on their wonderfully large dance floor. We truly enjoyed dancing together and, unlike many others who dance, had abounding fun.

"You don't love me like you used to, do you?" queried Mike.

"No," I painfully replied.

"We're kind of drifting apart, aren't we," Mike said.

"Yes," I agreed.

"I'm feeling the same," Mike said. "It seems the only thing we have in common is dancing."

I had to agree again.

"That's what's supposed to happen," I said. We were brought together to serve a purpose, and that purpose is almost fulfilled. I was to learn things from you, and you were to learn things from me. Then we are to drift apart and go on."

"We're almost at the end, aren't we," stated Mike empirically.

"Yes, we are."

"Why is that?" he asked. "Why have we drifted so far apart?"

"I've told you many times before, but you never wanted to listen."

"I'm ready now," he said. "Let's sit down."

We did, and I again tried to explain.

"Lifestyles," he said, trying to understand my statement.

"Yes, lifestyles." That seemed to say it all, but I continued. "You are not the kind of man I'm really looking for, because we are different. But remember, I'm not the kind of person you really need, either. I don't live the lifestyle you want to live, either. I'm not the one to make you really happy."

"I'll have to remember that," he said. "That's probably true. I don't have the same interests that you do. I have interests, but they're not the same as yours."

"That's right," I said. "And I want you to be happy. I really do."

"I want you to be happy, too. It's painful where we are headed," he added.

"I know."

"Understand that we have no more control over drifting apart than we did in meeting. You know very well that our meeting was created by a strong force, and not exactly by our own doing. We have no more control over it now than we did then."

"I'm just learning to understand," he said.

A pause took place in our conversation.

We decided to dance again, and let our thoughts settle.

"I still want you to go to my daughter's wedding with me," he said.

"Of course," I replied. The wedding was a few weeks away.

When we went back to my place for the night, we made love as usual, with all the warmth and tenderness that has always been there.

The following week brought the same care between us that had been there all along. We are just getting closer and more adjusted to the inevitable end.

Mike is not happy with the new job. It is very stressful, and he is not having any fun on the job at all.

Chapter Thirty-Nine

Laura's Wedding

It was a beautiful day, and also the day Mike's daughter, Laura, was getting married. We had been to the rehearsal dinner the night before, and I was pleased to find that her soon-to-be husband's family was delightful. She should be very happy.

I also had the pleasure of meeting Laura's mother, who was Mike's second wife. She was beautiful, as were all the others, but not one I could actually visualize with Mike. It seems that all of Mike's wives became heavy, but were very attractive. Laura has had a fight with weight herself, as did her lovely sister, Saundra. Still, they were all beautiful people, inside and out.

Since this was a Jewish wedding, I had a lot to learn. The customs were so different, and I had too often heard that Jewish people, women particularly, did not accept Gentiles too warmly. While they may not have been pleased that Mike was now introducing another shiksa, they were very kind to me.

I coached Mike on how to address the daughter he had not spoken to in many years. At their first catching sight of one another, there was an immediate tendency on the daughter's part to ignore him.

"Go up to her and tell her that it is very good to see her," I said.

He followed my suggestion.

The day went on, with no gesture of friendliness coming forth.

"Go tell her how lovely she looks," I coaxed him.

Again, he did as I said, getting a small smile from his daughter in return, but no more warmth than that.

Saundra had brought her daughter with her and was also accompanied by her husband, both of whom Mike had never met. He and the husband were able to carry on some conversation, and talked about the little girl as well. That seemed to ease some tension, but did not get a welcoming response at all from Saundra. She was still very distant.

"Make sure you let her know that you love her," I continued.

Mike had written a letter to Saundra and had brought it with him. He had left it in the car, but now felt it might be the right time to give it to her. He had asked me to read it earlier and tell him what I thought.

The letter was all about the anger he had carried in regard to his own father and how he had learned to let that go. He also explained that he understands that she has carried that same anger toward him, and that he hoped that she would also learn that it was not good to harbor those feelings. By his example, he hoped that

188

she, too, would forgive. I thought it was well written, and I urged him to ask her to please read it, since she had refused to accept mail from him in the past.

When he handed it to her, he told her she did not have to read it right away, but he asked her to please read it later when she felt ready. He also told her that he loved her.

"I know you do," she said, but there was no more giving on her part that was going to take place that day. She was going to keep her safe distance and keep herself protected from her pain. No matter what I said to her to try to warm the reception or soften the hardness that was there, there was a limit to how much she was going to soften at that time.

After the wedding, I asked Mike a few times if he had tried to make contact with her, but he had not. I don't think he felt that he could deal with the rejection, but I urged him to do so. I also knew that I was to stay in this relationship until he had the opportunity to meet face-to-face with her again.

I would do all that I could to help him straighten out this severely damaged relationship. I was there to support and encourage him, but he is the one who really understood the problem. He is the one who wrote his heartfelt feelings in the letter, and had harbored the same anger toward his father. He felt that the reasons for this same anger had been passed on from his father to him and from him to his daughter.

He now understood more clearly that he must also pass on this same understanding and ultimate forgiveness to her. My only hope was that in time his message would be understood and that they would work out their relationship.

Chapter Forty

Karmic Work Completed

More months have passed, and Mike and I are still dating. It is becoming more and more difficult to deal with not having any more than $10 to $15 an evening for entertainment. I am embarrassed to have him barter with the doorman over the cover charge to enjoy good music. He is so sweet and honest, that sometimes he gets us in for half price. This is not comfortable to me. Once we are in, I am confined to drinking a soft drink, water or coffee. I feel that we shouldn't even go.

Despite this hardship, I would never want to berate Mike about it. It is not his fault, as he is doing the best that he can. I just know that it isn't going to get any better; in fact, when the IRS makes their deal, it will probably get a lot worse. Still, Mike is mentally ready to pay his dues, and for someone who has not really ever faced responsibility, this is quite an accomplishment.

Besides the hardship of lack of funds, I am constantly reminded of the beauty that Mike sees in other women, particularly those who sing in the Motown bands. This is his true love in music, and he is enamored with the talent and exuberance of all female singers. While he appears to be truly loyal, the admiration is hurtful to me. It is not something I can overlook, as it has become obviously visible just too often. I feel he is showing his discontentment in the relationship, and I have inwardly held mine.

Mike and I each have an eye for beauty and visually appealing things or people. I remember one day when we had gone to a concert at a park, and there were some very girls on stage in full skirts and bobby socks doing a rock and roll show. He constantly admired these young ladies, commenting frequently on their looks.

"Which one to you think is the prettiest?" he queried.

"The little blond," I answered.

He agreed. But he wouldn't let it go. I didn't feel good that day anyway, so my patience with this was limited. He never said that he thought I was pretty, but he continued to look for beauty in all of the showgirls he encountered.

Again, he asked, "Which one of these girls do you think is the prettiest?"

I retorted with a hasty comment. I had had enough of his undying adulation of others for one day. It was not one of our more pleasant days.

His love of sports, which he tried to balance with his love of the relationship, began to show signs of the scales tipping. It was football season, and he would become engrossed in a game at home. Instead of coming over during halftime, he would not come over until after the game. He would apologize, and while I wasn't that upset by it, it was noted.

I still tried to assist with covering the cost of some of our entertainment when I could. There was a wedding to go to of one of my friends' children, so naturally I covered the cost of the gift. I also tried to pick up tickets for shows and plays so that it would not be obvious that I was carrying him for the evening.

On the weekend of the Saturday night wedding, I thought it would be nice to share more time with him and asked Mike if it would work out if I got tickets for a musical for Sunday afternoon, and he have visitation with his daughter after the show.

"Sure," he said. "If fact, I can probably move her to Monday."

Later the next day he said it was all worked out for us to have Saturday and Sunday together, and I purchased the tickets. I was quite pleased. I had even suggested that we stay overnight near the place of the wedding reception since it was in a city more than an hour away. We sometimes liked to do that, as he could usually use some points he had accumulated from sales to cover the cost of the room. That worked out pretty well for us.

The time grew near to the weekend. I think it was a Thursday night when I received a message on my answering machine.

"I'm really looking forward to us dancing the night away at the wedding Saturday, but I have a problem with Sunday. As you know, Ellie has been raised to make her own decisions, and she is not willing to give up her

Sunday afternoon. I will not be able to go with you on Sunday."

I was furious! As hard as I worked to keep the relationship going on limited funds, and worked to see that we had some variety of entertainment, and he was going to let some little four year old dictate his plans! I was not going to tolerate any youngster rearranging my schedule when there was no significant reason. That was NOT going to work for me.

I left him a message back saying, "That's okay, I'll take care of using the tickets, but if it were a football game, I bet you'd work it out!"

I did not get a call until the next day. It was a message asking me to call him back.

When I did, he seemed a little unsettled, and choked up, but managed to say, "I don't think we should see each other anymore."

"I'm getting to that point, too, Mike."

In truth, I was letting the relationship drag on until we went to this wedding; but then, I'm not sure I would have done anything about it anyway.

"Well, I don't think there's any more we can say to each other at this point."

"No, I don't suppose so."

"I hope there are no hard feelings," Mike said.

"No, there aren't. Not at all," I replied. "You're too sweet for that."

"There aren't any here, either," he said.

There honestly were not any hard feelings on either of our parts, and we said good bye. That was the simplest breakup I have ever had. I missed him for quite a while, but I knew it was the right thing to have happen. It was the right time, and it happened just when it was supposed to.

I later said to Gwenn, "That was the least painful breakup I have ever gone through. I am not angry with him, nor do I dislike him. I have very warm thoughts about the man."

"That's because you have completed whatever purpose you were to complete, and now it is time to move on. You knew that right from the start."

"Yes, I did. But why did I have to love him?"

"If you didn't, you never would have tolerated him," she said.

"You must be right. I never would have."

Dance, Dance, Dance

Mike called today. This is the first we have spoken in a year and a half. I've thought about him many times and more than once tried to contact him. All points of contact for him had changed, so I was unsuccessful. We always loved to dance. He asked me to go dancing with him, and I accepted.

February 19, 2001

Epilogue

Mike had called early one Monday morning, about a year and a half after we had ended our relationship. We agreed we would go dancing on Friday night.

That entire day and the next few days were filled with thoughts of Mike. I hadn't realized that I still very much loved him. Even though my head told me this was very wrong and that I couldn't enter into a relationship with him, I very much wanted to be with him. I wanted to express every form of love that I could with him. I still loved him.

I learned something quite important at this point in my life. My heart sang. Life took on new meaning. Everything I did brought forth thoughts of Mike. Everything I saw in a store to buy was more fulfilling because of the love-sharing feelings I had for Mike. I was happy at a level I had forgotten existed; I had thought I was very happy with my life prior to his call. This was a profound realization. I was making wonderful mental plans with this man, and my heart raced with fulfilling thoughts. I even entertained how I might make this relationship work for us.

Mike was the most uplifting, kind and thoughtful man I had ever known. No matter what hardship he was besieged with, his spirit lifted him. What a gift he has. What he lacks in manhood, he exudes in personality. He becomes my sole lifeline to happiness. I clearly recalled my experience of this with him.

An extraordinary realization to me was how those feelings had laid dormant in my heart, while the level of joy I felt in my life was missing this height of real happiness. I considered my life to be quite happy, as I didn't need anyone to make my life full. What I didn't realize was the amount of love I have to share and have no one worthy of that love in my life. This was a profound happiness beyond my own total happiness. How could I have forgotten how that felt?

The Thursday preceding our date, I received a telephone message from Mike. He had called to cancel our date because he had gone back with his girlfriend. My first reaction was to be relieved. I knew that this would not be good for us to begin anew, and I knew I would not and could not resist him. I yearned for him. I reveled in the thoughts of him, the fun we had together, and the joy we shared.

My second reaction was disappointment, and the third heartbreak. I had no idea that I still loved this man, yet alone how deeply. I was immersed in emotion for him and astounded at the reality of this.

I have faulted Mike for his lack of being a man, and his inability to physically care for and protect his mate. I could not accept that he was incapable of providing the real roots of a home and homestead, nor the desire. Taking care of Mike was all he could do. To offset his faults, he is quite spiritually and emotionally mature in regard to feelings and relationships. He should be commended for his handling of these affairs. What he does cradle with care are your feelings. He has honorable human qualities of honesty, loyalty, sharing and kindness that few men can match. His uplifting spirit carries him high at all times.

I did not respond to his message. I felt that no contact would be better. I listened to the tape-recorded message he left for me again. I could hear that he was happy to have worked it out with his lady friend, and that pleased me. It took away most of my pain. That is love.

www.ingramcontent.com/pod-product-compliance
Lightning Source LLC
Chambersburg PA
CBHW072000040426
42447CB00009B/1415